# THE
# LITTLE BOOK OF
# BIG
# EXPENSES

# THE
# LITTLE BOOK OF
# BIG
# EXP£NSES

## HOW TO LIVE
## THE MP LIFESTYLE

A&C Black • London

Published 2009 by A & C Black Publishers Limited

36 Soho Square, London W1D 3QY

www.acblack.com

ISBN: 978-1-4081-2404-8

Copyright © A&C Black Publishers Limited, 2009

*Produced by* Heritage Editorial: heritage2ed@aol.com

*Designed by* Trevor Bounford: studio@bounford.com

A CIP catalogue record for this book is available from the British Library.

This book is produced using paper that is made from wood grown in managed, sustainable forests. It is natural, renewable and recyclable. The logging and manufacturing processes conform to the environmental regulations of the country of origin.

Printed and bound in Great Britain by Clays Ltd., St. Ives plc.

*Picture credits:*
graphics by studio@bounford.com; original cartoons from a private collection.

# CONTENTS

# FOREWORD

**The Little Book of Big Expenses**

It may well go down in history as the Summer of Discomfort. In May 2009, as Britain bathed under blue skies Britain's Right Honourable Members of Parliament were feeling a different kind of heat. The Freedom of Information Act was introduced by the Labour government in 2004 but, unfortunately, the much vaunted step forward turned out to be a serious shot in the foot. The Act ensured anything that involved the public or the expenditure of its money in the form of taxpayers money, was now held to be in the 'public domain' and open for scrutiny by all and sundry, from the closeted offices of auditors, the judiciary and the police, to members of the public. *The Daily Telegraph* brought an action in 2006 demanding that MPs' expenses be made public and, after much prevarication and numerous delaying tactics it was agreed that the full claims would be made available in mid-July 2009 – not long before the Summer parliamentary recess. But then the *Telegraph* pounced – or rather, scooped.

**Bloodbath over Breakfast**

The full expense accounts were leaked to the newspaper, and on Friday 8th May the *Telegraph* began to publish an unprecedented run of shocking revelations about those who govern the UK. Lurid tales of greed, penny-pinching, fraud and, ultimately, appalling incompetence outraged, enthralled and amused the public. Many of the expense claims made by the UK's 646 MPs were completely legitimate, and most were 'within the rules' as MPs were quick to claim. But if you mix up your dirty washing, the dye usually runs. From members of the Cabinet to the most distant backbenchers, few were untainted. Some MPs fell on their swords almost immediately and Scotland Yard announced they would be investigating some of the more outrageous expense claims. Others jumped before they were pushed.

And this is why...

# PART ONE:
# A CAN OF WORMS

"We were only following the rules", said UK MPs caught up in the Great Expenses Scandal of 2009. But the defence has a hollow ring. After all, our politicians did draw up the rules themselves. Even so, many of them seem to have had a hard time following them.

# THE RULES

The Bible of MPs' expense claims is *The Green Book – A Guide to Members' Allowances*, published by the House of Commons in March 2009. In his foreword, the soon to be ousted Speaker Michael Martin reminds readers that 'the text has been agreed by members of the House'. Perhaps significantly, he refrains from reiterating the warning made in his introduction to the 2006 edition that 'Members themselves are responsible for ensuring that their use of allowances is above reproach'.

Before we judge our parliamentary comrades for their liberal interpretations of the expenses rules, let's see just how complicated this crucial manual is. Right at the beginning, *The Green Book* spells out what parliamentary allowances are actually *for*:

Members of Parliament are provided with financial support in the form of allowances to enable them to work effectively in Parliament and in their constituencies. Parliamentary allowances are designed to ensure that Members are reimbursed for costs properly incurred in the performance of their duties. They provide support for:

- Employing staff (Staffing Expenditure)

- Provision of facilities, equipment and supplies for themselves and their staff (Administrative and Office Expenditure)

- Overnight stays away from home whilst on parliamentary duties (Personal Additional Accommodation Expenditure)

- Communicating with constituents (Communications Expenditure)

- House stationery and postage (Stationery and Postage)

- Travel between Westminster, the constituency and main home (Travel Expenditure)

### Guidelines
The book then goes on to enumerate the fundamental principles that govern the expenses regime, which are derived from the 1995 *Code of Conduct for Members of Parliament*. They

are based, we are told, 'on concepts of selflessness, integrity, objectivity, accountability, openness, honesty and leadership'. Key principles include:

- Claims should be above reproach and must reflect actual usage of the resources being claimed.

- Claims must only be made for expenditure that it was necessary for a Member to incur to ensure that he or she could properly perform his or her parliamentary duties.

- It is not permissible for a Member to claim under any parliamentary allowance for anything that the Member is claiming from any other source.

- Members must ensure that claims do not give rise to, or give the appearance of giving rise to, an improper personal financial benefit to themselves or anyone else.

- Members are committed to openness about what expenditure has been incurred and for what purposes.

- Individual Members take personal responsibility for all expenses incurred, for making claims and for keeping records, even if the administration of claims is delegated by them to others.

- The requirement of ensuring value for money is central in claiming for accommodation, goods or services – Members should avoid purchases which could be seen as extravagant or luxurious.

### Finally...

In case some Members are still in the dark, *The Green Book* outlines a series of questions for them to ask themselves when contemplating making an expenses claim:

- Is this expense genuinely incurred by me in my role as a Member of Parliament as opposed to my personal capacity?

- Is this purchase supporting me in carrying out my parliamentary duties?

- Could the claim in any way damage the reputation of Parliament or its Members?

- How comfortable do I feel with the knowledge that my claim will be available to the public under Freedom of Information?

At last we see where *The Green Book* came a cropper. It failed to spell out what MPs should do when the answers were 'no', 'no', 'yes' and 'not very'.

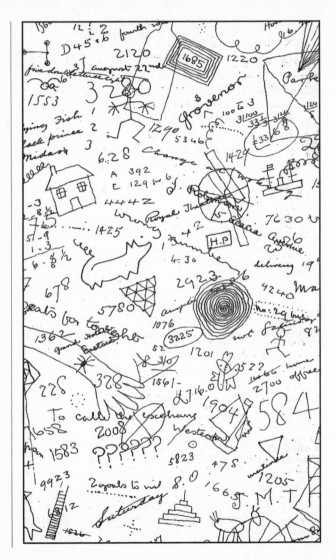

**The Little Book of Big Expenses**

# KEEPING TRACK

If you are a busy politician, constantly meeting the demands of your party, your constituents and pursuing any other occupation you may have, then the mundane task of keeping an accurate record of the innumerable day-to-day expenses you might run up and be entitled to must often feel like one job too many. But when you are likely to be stuck on a miserly basic of £64,766 per annum, getting back what you are entitled to according to *The Green Book* rapidly becomes a top priority.

No wonder, then, that occasional mistakes are made.

The unfortunate **Phil Woolas**, the Immigration Minister (ministerial salary, £105,412) obviously had far too much on his plate keeping job-hungry foreigners at bay. While back in 2004 the monthly food allowance was £400, and claims did not need to be backed up by receipts, Mr. Woolas normally claimed less than his food allowance, and did "as a matter of transparency" submit receipts from Tesco, Sainsbury's and other popular supermarket chains. In all fairness, his honesty was his problem, as an eagle-eyed clerk at the Fees Office spotted a number of interesting inedible items, including nail polish, women's shoes and a jumper, disposable nappies, baby wipes, comics, panty liners, tampons and other domestic necessities, plus an unallowable (or is that unswallowable?) £3.49 bottle of plonk.*

Mr. Woolas' unlucky oversights were exactly that – oversights. What remains astonishing are the innumerable 'oversights' which *did* slip through the Fees Office net, but with a (current) golden carrot of £24,006 just on the 'second home' Additional Costs Allowance dangling in front of them, some MPs might almost be forgiven for making asses of themselves. Some might simply appear greedy. And more than a few seem downright devious.

*Unfortunately, however, on several occasions Mr. Woolas had to be reminded by Commons officials that £400 per month on food was indeed the upper limit allowed.

# AN A-Z OF MP's EXPENSES

By way of an introduction to the *smörgåsbord* of items listed among MPs' claims to be found in later pages, here is a quick taster.

| | | | |
|---|---|---|---|
| A | Automatic gates | £4,936 | Jonathan Djanogly (*Con*) |
| B | Box of Matches | 59p | John Greenway (*Con*) |
| C | Chopping board | £1.75 | Jo Swinson (*Lib Dem*) |
| D | Dog bowl | £2.99 | Mike Penning (*Con*) |
| E | Elephant lamps | £134.30 | Michael Gove (*Con*) |
| F | Fine art insurance premium | £937 | Barbara Follett (*Lab*) |
| G | Glasses – pair of | £210 | Michael Clapham (*Lab*) |
| H | Helipad – trimming of hedge around | £609 | Michael Spicer (*Con*) |
| I | Ice-cube tray | £1.50 | John Reid (*Lab*) |
| J | Jaffa Cakes | £1.60 | Mark Francois (*Con*) |
| K | Kenyan carpets – pair of | £200 | Bob Marshall Andrews (*Lab*) |
| L | Leather rocking chair | £1,200 | Julia Goldsworthy (*Lib Dem*) |

| | | | |  |
|---|---|---|---|---|
| $\mathcal{M}$ | Massage chair | £730 | Shahid Malik (*Lab*) | |
| $\mathcal{N}$ | Nappies | £5.65 | Phil Woolas (*Lab*) | |
| $\mathcal{O}$ | Odd jobs | £2,191 | David Willetts (*Con*) | |
| $\mathcal{P}$ | Piano tuning | £40 | Douglas Hogg (*Con*) | |
| $\mathcal{Q}$ | Quiche dish (part of dinner set) | £155 | Unnamed Labour MP | |
| $\mathcal{R}$ | Rentokil | £352 | Gordon Brown (*Lab*) | |
| $\mathcal{S}$ | Shed base | £750 | David Willetts (*Con*) | |
| $\mathcal{T}$ | Trouser press | £119 | Chris Huhne (*Lib Dem*) | |
| $\mathcal{U}$ | Umbrella (House of Commons brand) | £14.50 | Claire Curtis Thomas (*Lab*) | |
| $\mathcal{V}$ | Video rental* | £10 | Jacqui Smith (*Lab*)** | |
| $\mathcal{W}$ | Windows XP for Dummies | £16.99*** | Kenneth Clarke (*Con*) | |
| $\mathcal{X}$ | Xmas decorations, including two trees | £286 | Vera Baird (*Lab*) | |
| $\mathcal{Y}$ | Yucca plant | £9.99 | Unnamed Lib Dem MP | |
| $\mathcal{Z}$ | Zanussi fridge-freezer | £199 | Derek Conway (*Independent*) | |

* For anyone who thinks that the public has been unforgivably kept in the dark about the precise nature of Jacqui Smith's husband's porno flicks, we can reveal that the titles available at the time on the couple's TV package at the time were *Raw Meat 3* and *By Special Request*.

** This claim, as was immediately made clear by the then Home Secretary, was an unfortunate oversight.

*** Recommended Retail Price.

# PROPERTY PORTFOLIOS

The British are famously obsessed with property, and the nation's politicians are no exception. In previous years, as house prices shot through the roof, our MPs saw no good reason to refrain from jumping on the bandwagon. Indeed, many of them may have felt that they owed it to themselves, Parliament having played a key role in allowing the bubble to inflate in the first place. And it might have been the bursting of that particular bubble that helped to reveal the dry rot at the foundation of the parliamentary expenses system.

*"I don't care what you're asking for it. After all, I'm not paying".*

There is no doubt that the single greatest use (and abuse) of the Fees Office's resources has been on housing of one sort or another. Aided by generous 'second home' allowances, some MPs have played the real estate game with a shamelessness that would make Sarah Beeny blush.

Designations of second homes have been changed (by) left, right and centre, prompting cynics to suggest that the proprietors might even have been trying to milk the system. (The fact that the Inland Revenue has not been party to some of these switches has done little to dampen such speculation).

Husband and wife teams have been busted for both claiming mortgage interest on the same property. Speculation on the housing market was unabashedly unrestrained – switching 'first' and 'second' home designations after expensive refurbishment being the most popular and money-making ruse. Glamorous fixtures and fittings have appeared in MPs' crash pads, and gardens have bloomed at the taxpayers' expense.

Meanwhile, the country has developed a whole new lexicon. If asked what 'dippers' and 'flippers' were beforehand, most of us would either have 'passed' or tentatively suggested that they might be birds.

Such innocence has gone forever.

# FLIPPING 'ECK...

For MPs with more than two houses, the business of deciding which is your 'main home' and which of the others is your 'second home' can be tricky. Even more complicated is working out which second home you are claiming expenses for under ACA (and therefore where to have that nice new sofa delivered). With the awkward business of Capital Gains Tax to factor in as well, it's easy to become befuddled.

**Ed Balls** and **Yvette Cooper** (*Lab*). Prior to Mr. Balls' election as MP for Normanton in 2005, Ms. Cooper had been claiming a modest £530 a month for mortgage interest on her Yorkshire home. Once they both needed to spend time in Westminster, however, they flipped to a South London property, claiming £733 each against mortgage interest. In 2007, they flipped again, to a larger house in North London on which they claimed just over £1,031 each. Confused? They were. In 2006, they were warned by the fees office that they had submitted same claim twice, and again in 2008 investigated for designating the house they lived in during the week as their second home. In a valiant attempt to shed light on the matter, the couple explained: "We did move house in London. But in the two years following our move, we have claimed less than in the two years prior to our move".

**Margaret Moran** (*Lab*). Poor Margaret Moran has had quite a time of it rushing between Westminster, her constituency and her husband. Over a period of four years she flipped her designated second home three times. The first property was a flat near the House of Commons, to which she added a new kitchen (£4,756.40) and carpet (£2,678). The following year she designated her constituency house in Luton as her second home, doing up the garden (£2,350) and bathroom (£1,823.09) before embarking on general maintenance (a further £1,207.50 plus £4,200 for decorators). Eyebrows began to rise in Westminster, however, when she subsequently flipped to her husband's house in Southampton, despite it being 100 miles away and riddled with dry rot. The fungus was promptly treated at a cost of £22,500 and the bill submitted to the Fees Office, who initially queried it as "appearing to be against the spirit of allowances", before coughing up the full amount on the grounds that "there was nothing with regard to the rules that we could pull the claim on".

**Hazel Blears** (*Lab*), whose brief as Communities Secretary gave her control of housing policy, might be expected to be a little more savvy than most about matters pertaining to her own properties. Within just one year, Ms. Blears declared three separate properties as her second home. The first, in March 2004, was her constituency house in Salford, for which she claimed £850 for a TV and video and £651 for a mattress. Just one month later, she flipped to a flat in Kennington, claiming £850 per month mortgage interest against it. In August of the same year, she sold the flat at a profit of £45,000 before buying another London flat in December. This too was designated her second home, and mortgage costs of £1,000 a month were billed to the Fees Office, plus expense claims for furniture and another new TV.

Where Ms. Blears came a cropper though, was when she failed to pay around £18,000 Capital Gains Tax on the profit made from selling the first London flat, in her confusion having informed the Inland Revenue that it was, in fact, her main residence. Blaming the Fees Office for her original designation, and feeling very much a victim of circumstances beyond her control, Ms. Blears commented: "I understand entirely why the public hates this. The system is wrong, it needs to be changed".

**Michael Gove** (*Con*) originally designated his North Kensington house as his second home. In May 2006, he reallocated it as his main home. And no wonder; over a period of a few months during the first half of 2006 he had lavished £7,000 of taxpayers' money on it, around 30% of which was on gorgeous fittings from Oka Direct, the interiors company established by David Cameron's posh mother-in-law. A man of international tastes, items acquired included a Manchu cabinet (£493), a Loire table (£750) and a pair of 'elephant lamps' (£134.50). In September 2006, Mr. Gove acquired a £395,000 second second home in Surrey (although he now no longer had his first second home). He claimed £13,259 for the cost of moving to this new house and, over the periods 2006-07 and 2007-08 submitted bills to the maximum amount allowable under the ACA. When his expenses came to light, Mr. Gove issued a lengthy statement in which he confessed: "I realize that the costs of several individual items of furniture I bought could have been lower and I understand why that is a matter of criticism", but described allegations that he had flipped as "misleading".

**Tory Stories**
The Shadow Secretary for Health, squeaky-clean Member for South Cambridgeshire **Andrew Lansley**, got his fingers burnt over property when the restoration of his designated thatched Tudor second home in the village of Melbourn was complete. He promptly flipped the property, and it went on the market, the family shifting their home base to the nearby family-friendly village of Orwell, while his second home became a Georgian flat in London, subsequently sumptuously done over as well. Another interesting right-of-centre flipper includes Tory old-timer **Francis Maude**, Shadow Minister for the Foreign Office. Having already got his Sussex main home/London second home mortgage payments in a twist, Maude proceeded to buy a flat a few minutes walk around the corner from the home he already owned in London. He then rented his original London property out, thus allowing the taxpayer to pay the mortgage interest on his 'new' second home.

**The Little Book of Big Expenses**

### Carefully Doing Their Sums

You couldn't fit a cigarette paper between contenders for the Exchequer hot seat, Labour incumbent **Alistair Darling** and his shadow **George Osborne**, when it comes to nest-feathering (or incompetence at basic maths). Mr. Darling is a serial flipper, cleverly switching his main and second homes between London and his constituency in Edinburgh four times in two years to maximize on allowances – but all "within the rules". Similarly his potential nemesis, Mr. Osborne, who bought a farmhouse to be near his Tatton constituency in Cheshire (ten months before he actually won the seat) avoided a mortgage on his new rural retreat by remortgaging his London town house. After winning Tatton, the farmhouse was 'flipped' to become his second home, taking out a mortgage on it, thereby reducing that on his Notting Hill Gate home, which he subsequently sold for £1.45 million – at a profit of £748,000. Delighted by their windfall, the Osbornes moved a few yards down the road, presumably to repeat the cash-harvesting exercise.

**Gordon Brown** (*Lab*), on the other hand, shows how it should be done. Most people would regard having a grace-and-favour apartment in Downing Street as a bit of a perk. Gordon Brown though seems to have taken a while to get used to the idea, or maybe he just didn't like the neighbours. As Chancellor, he declined the more glamorous address in favour of a modest bolthole less than a mile away which he designated as his second home. Being more aware than most of the need to keep taxpayer costs to a minimum, the flat was refurbished simply with an Ikea kitchen, a mere snip at £9,000, and the cleaner was shared with his brother. Ten days after Tony Blair announced his intention to resign as Prime Minister, however, Mr. Brown had a change of heart: Downing Street would do after all. He generously gave the Westminster flat to his wife and flipped his second home to a property in Fife, claiming for cleaning, gardening and plumbing services against it.

# SHOW ME THE WAY TO GO HOME

If you are a geographically-challenged MP, remembering exactly where your various homes are can be decidedly tricky. The Additional Costs Allowance (ACA) was designed, quite reasonably, to allow those members whose constituencies were far removed from Westminster to attend Parliamentary sittings regularly. However, the publication of MPs' expenses drawn against the ACA revealed an intriguing network of 'safe houses' and alternative addresses reminiscent of the underground resistance in Europe during the Second World War.

**James Clappison** (*Con*) seems to have got the hang of it. Despite owning a phenomenal 24 houses, he was still able to remember which one he could use to claim over £100,000 in expenses. At the other end of the scale, **Laura Moffatt** (*Lab*) admirably solved the problem altogether by giving up her London flat and installing a camp bed in her office.

Nevertheless, quite a few of their less astute colleagues have managed to get themselves into a right old tangle about where they actually live. Which house is which, they cry, and does it even have to be a house in the traditional sense?

## Clubland

When **John Mann** (*Lab*) described Parliament as a 'gentlemen's club' he was not far from the truth. Indeed, a number of his colleagues so relished the club-like atmosphere of their workplace that they took up residence at some of London's most exclusive private members' clubs. A home from home, they might say. Deputy Conservative Party Chairman **John Maples** found the RAC club in Pall Mall much to his taste and wasted no time designating it as his main home for a period, during which he also claimed the maximum second home costs allowable against his house in Oxfordshire.

The Garrick Club in the heart of London's theatre district, founded 'for the purpose of combining the use of a Club, on economic principles, with the advantages of a literary society', was author and journalist **Michael Gove**'s preferred haunt. Mr. Gove (*Con*) charged the public purse £500 for overnight stays at the illustrious edifice, just a couple of miles from his family house in North Kensington. (*See also* **Homes for Cash**).

**John Hayes** (*Con*) preferred to lay down his head at that 'oldest, most elite, and most important of all Conservative clubs', the Carlton Club in St James's Street, where overnight costs start at £121 for a standard single room.

**Angus McNeil** (*SNP*), having unfortunately "left my keys in the Hebrides" sought out "the cheapest hotel I could find" and presented the Fees Office with a bill for two nights at the Union Jack Club in Waterloo. Odd choice for a separatist.

### The Stay-at-Home Generation
Sadly, the costs of getting onto the property ladder these days mean that many young people are unable to leave the family home until they are well into adulthood. Some folk, however, find it hard to cut those childhood ties even when they have perfectly good (second) homes of their own, not to mention a well-paid job. Quite frankly, they should be old enough to stand on their own two feet.

Labour minister **Baroness Thornton**, 56, still regards her mother's modest bungalow in Yorkshire as her main home, although she occasionally joins her husband and children at their house in Belsize Park. Since 2002, the Baroness has claimed £130,000 in expenses against the London property.

**Tony McNulty** (*Lab*) still hankers after his mother's cooking at the age of 50. Mr. McNulty designated his parents' house

*"Excuse me occifer, but will I get a receipt for this in the morning?"*

in Harrow as his main home while charging the taxpayer £60,000 for his second, which lies not ten miles away in Hammersmith.

**Fabian Hamilton** (*Lab*) claimed to have spent the majority of his time with his mother at her London house prior to her death in 2005. He also had a family home of his own in Leeds against which he claimed not only mortgage interest, as permitted under the ACA, but also the full repayment costs, overcharging by almost £3,000 before the Fees Office discovered the error in 2004.

For **Jacqui Smith** (*Lab*), it was a sibling tie that proved strongest. Sisters have been known to squabble over who owns what, and so it was that a terrace house in London came to be designated as Ms. Smith's main residence despite being technically owned by her sister, Sara. Meanwhile, the former

Home Secretary was able to claim £116,000 in second home expenses against the house she did actually own herself, her constituency home in Redditch.

## Address Unknown

For time-pressed MPs, the business of shopping for furnishings for their second home can be a major chore, what with the palaver of finding the right sofa, remembering which house it's for and arranging delivery. Perhaps understandably, not all of them get it quite right all of the time.

**Madeleine Moon** (*Lab*), MP for Bridgend, has a second home in London as well as a house in Wales. Ever mindful of the need to support businesses local to her constituency, she spent more than £4,000 on furniture in Wales under the allowance for her London property. Speaking for Welsh multiple home-owners everywhere, the patriotic MP explained: "The Welsh shop in Wales, even when it is for installation in London".

**Robert Syms** (*Con*) meanwhile, appeared to have become altogether disorientated about the whereabouts of his second home in London when he ordered £2,000 worth of furniture on expenses and gave instruction for it to be delivered to his parents' house in Wiltshire. He subsequently explained that he had been far too busy to sit around waiting for it to turn up, but that the furniture had been duly transferred to the correct address. "My parents took delivery and then I took it up to London a week or two later to my second address – I drove the van myself", he added proudly. **Ed Vaizey** (*Con*) got in a similar muddle. He claimed over £2,000 for furniture for his second home in Oxford but had it delivered to his London address. Perhaps Robert Syms would be kind enough to lease him his (presumably white) van, after all. One or the other could claim the cost back from the Fees Office.

# HOMES FOR CASH

The Houses of Parliament have often been likened to a 'Gentlemen's club'. One outraged correspondent to *The Times* angrily dismissed this, pointing out that any MP who had abused his expenses could hardly be classed as a 'gentleman', and would, if already a member, be blackballed or, if applying for membership, would be refused.

Whither, then, the clubbable future of Garrick member, Tory whip and noted Eurosceptic, **Bill Cash** the Conservative member for Stone?

No doubt frequently tired and emotional upon leaving either of his 'clubs' after a hard day's grind, Mr. Cash appears to have neatly solved the problem of how to navigate his way back to his second home (his main home being a 16th-century rural pile in Shropshire) by having several:

- His designated second home early in 2005 was a flat in Notting Hill owned by his striking 'Oxford set' daughter, high-flying prospective Tory candidate Laetitia. He subsequently agreed to pay back the £15,000 he claimed that year for the rent he paid to Laetitia, who later sold the flat at a £48,000 profit.

- In the meantime, a 'modest' flat he already owned in Pimlico (a few minutes walk from Parliament) was inconveniently occupied by his son – rent-free. In August 2005, Mr. Cash designated this as his second home, despite it having "no bath, and no bath plug".

- However, during Summer 2005, Cash also claimed for frequent overnight stays at the Carlton Hotel, just around the corner from his Pimlico flat. When voyaging the 1.5 miles to the Carlton seemed simply a step too far, Mr. Cash also resorted to the members' accommodation at the Garrick, billing nearly £2,500 to the taxpayer.

### ... Owzat! Out for a Duck

Introduced to Sir Mick Jagger by Laetitia at a wedding in 2003, Mr. Cash (no doubt seizing on the opportunity of having a genuine Stone on the Stone batting side) tried to engage the ageing 'national rock treasure' and cricket enthusiast on the issue of the European single currency.

The response: "I hope you don't think I'm being rude, but would you just piss off?"

*"... and then he said he'd been told there weren't any rooms available upstairs, so could he kip on the sofa at my place?"*

# BIG DIPPERS

**MPs are not allowed to claim expenses against more than one second property at a time. Fairly straightforward, you'd think. But for dippers with a number of properties it is all too easy to lose track of which house they are claiming against. Then there's the question of working from one's home 'office'. And how are dipper couples to avoid becoming double-dippers? It's a minefield out there. Below are just a few who have come a cropper. Are they guilty? You decide.**

As Chancellor of the Exchequer, **Alistair Darling** (*Lab*) knows all about putting money back into the economy: it's part of his job. He found himself having to return a little more than he bargained for, however, when investigations revealed that he had been claiming expenses against his nominated second home while simultaneously recovering costs for his grace-and-favour apartment in Downing Street. With four second homes in as many years – Mr. Darling was also a serial flipper – it is perhaps not surprising that he felt the need to call in a professional to manage his own financial affairs, charging the public purse £1,400 for an accountant.

**Malcom Bruce** (*Lib Dem*) was able to claim thousands against both his second home London flat and his constituency property just outside Gordon in north-east Scotland. How did he do it? Well, it just happened that his office manager, diary secretary and wife are one and the same person and she prefers to work north of the border. Mr. Bruce was therefore able to claim for office costs against the Scottish property under the Incidental Expenditure Provision. You might wonder why Mrs. Bruce doesn't work out of his constituency office, just 22 miles away in Inverurie. Mr. Bruce, clearly a hard taskmaster, explains that "home working enables my wife to ... be at her desk earlier". One hopes she is allowed to pop out for a sandwich at lunchtime.

*"Oh, be practical, darling. If I'm up here, and you're down there, well, where the hell is the cat going to live?"*

**Derek Conway** (*Con*) – the troubled Tory MP, despite having designated a flat in London as his second home, claimed that his parliamentary 'office' was a property in Morpeth. And that's not all he claimed. 'Office expenses' funded from the public purse included a £199 fridge-freezer and a £399 SatNav device, no doubt for finding his way back to his London constituency a mere 330-mile commute away.

**Sir Alan Beith** (*Lib Dem*) and **Baroness Maddock**. Sir Alan, knighted in 2008 for services to politics, put himself forward in May 2009 for the post of Speaker, pledging that he was

"willing to take on the task of leading reform". At the time Chairman of the Justice Committee of the House of Commons, as well as being a committed Christian and Methodist Lay Preacher, one would hope that his moral compass would point the right way. The couple, however, could do with a few maths lessons before he steps into the breach. Between 2001 and 2008, he claimed £117,750 in allowances for his second home, whilst in the same period his wife claimed £60,000 for overnight subsistence as permitted under House of Lords expenses, for the same address. Lady Maddock explained: "We have tried to claim half and half. I have always claimed half of what I could claim for and Alan only claims for half the rent. It isn't an exact science". Clearly, the problem lies in working with complex fractions: "We could have worked out the half much more accurately perhaps, but we did our best", she added.

**Andrew MacKay** and **Julie Kirkbride** (both *Con*) kept things simpler. Rather than both trying to claim on the same property, he claimed over £1,000 a month mortgage interest against their London property as his second home, while she designated her constituency flat in Bromsgrove as her second home and likewise claimed £900 mortgage expenses there. Having checked the arrangement with the Fees Office back in 1997 and been given full approval by its most senior official, the pair were understandably confident that they were doing nothing wrong. Mr. MacKay, on submitting his expenses file to David Cameron, even joked: "No swimming pools there". It was possibly his last laugh. Party officials deemed the set-up as failing the 'reasonableness' criteria set by Mr. Cameron, and Mr. MacKay resigned immediately. Ms. Kirkbride struggled on, buoyed by the "very humbling" trust of local supporters, although she declined to meet her constituents and over 3,500 of them signed a petition for her to go. When it was disclosed that she had claimed a further £50,000 for an extension to her second property to house her brother, however, it was the end of the road for Ms. Kirkbride.

**Taken to the Cleaners**

Not strictly 'dipping', but an interesting variant on the scam was developed by the five (only) MPs of a particular party that has only been able to sit at Westminster since 2001.

Organize the steps you need to take to successfully operate the scam in the correct order and then, for a bonus point, guess the party involved. Answers in a brown paper parcel please:*

- Rent three London properties (from the same landlord) using the ACA.
- Get elected to Westminster.
- Claim to "regularly travel to London to work".
- Avoid being seen by any neighbours or property managers.
- Claim rents on properties above the market rate.
- Proclaim that any association with unlawful activities is a thing of the past.
- When actually in London, shuffle the three addresses available for you to stay in.
- Do not attend the House of Commons.
- Ensure all receipts submitted to the Fees Office are rudimentary, preferably hand-written with no business address supplied.
- Claim on the ACA for two 'Samson' (*sic*)** 28-inch TVs (£329 a pop), DVD Sony cinema surround systems, a £795 cosy three-seater sofa, and a whopping £485 for Venetian blinds (presumably so nobody can see what you're up to).
- Spend a lot of time in a Province (*sic*).

*For super-bonus points can you name the five MPs involved?

** Please ignore this editorial intrusion if it makes the quiz too easy.

# MORTGAGE, WHAT MORTGAGE?

Pity those anxious MPs who are kept awake at night by overestimating the amount they owe on their mortgages. More unfortunate still are those that have received visitations from that terrifying spectre – the phantom mortgage. Here are some of the most haunted.

**Michael Fallon** (*Con*), ever quick to criticize the banking sector for excesses such as overpayment, wasted no time in firing off a stern note to the Fees Office when it was discovered that he himself had been overpaid for his mortgage expenses to the tune of £8,300. It turned out that Mr. Fallon had claimed for his capital repayments as well as the interest. "Why has no one brought this to my attention before?" he thundered, before setting about readdressing at least part of the imbalance by paying back £2,200. The remaining £6,100 was offset against his allowance.

**Bill Wiggin** (*Con*) submitted no less than 23 separate mortgage claims against a house on which he had no mortgage at all, collecting a total of £11,000 in just under two years. "I think people need to realize we are but human", Mr. Wiggin pleaded, adding hopefully "I am sure plenty of people have got the forms wrong". His leader, somewhat less forgiving of human error, condemned the overcharge as a "bad mistake".

Poor **David Chaytor** (*Lab*) spent a whole year labouring under the delusion that he still had to pay £1,175 a month for his Westminster flat. Failing to register that the mortgage had been entirely paid off by January 2004, between September 2005 and August 2006 Mr. Chaytor claimed nearly £13,000 in mortgage interest under his second home allowance. Mr. Chaytor has since stepped down from the Labour party.

**Elliot Morley** (*Lab*) was another who missed the chance to celebrate the moment when he became mortgage-free, claiming £16,000 worth of interest over 18 months before the oversight was spotted. Feeling more hard done-by than most of us might after receiving such a windfall, a contrite Mr. Morley said "I have made a mistake... and if I suffer financially as a result of that, I have only myself to blame".

**Ben Chapman**'s (*Lab*) mortgage on his second home in Lambeth was a hefty £380,000, leading him to claim back interest payments of £1,900 a month. After selling "some small properties" Mr. Chapman found himself with the enviable dilemma of "either using the receipts to purchase other properties or, which was for me a bit more comfortable, to pay off some of the mortgage". He duly opted for the latter, and his monthly interest payments plummeted to £398. Unused to this new level of comfort, Mr. Chapman continued to claim the full £1,900 a month he originally owed, benefiting to the tune of around £15,000 at public expense. To the unrepentant Chapman this was only fair; by choosing to reduce his mortgage he was, after all, "forgoing interest and investment opportunities elsewhere". He needn't have worried: the authorities are now paying him plenty of interest.

For **Shailesh Vara** (*Con*), it was the timing of his mortgage payments that caused the problem. Following his election to Parliament in May 2005, Mr Vara lodged mortgage interest claims of £1,174.13 for the period before he became an MP. When called to account, he accused his critics of "putting two and two together and making five". Mr. Vara might be wiser to consider his own mathematical shortcomings.

# SNAKES AND
# PROPERTY LADDERS

The booming housing market of the past few years has been kind to our MPs, particularly those who have bought, sold or 'flipped' second homes in central London. A lucky few have managed to leap so many rungs up the property ladder that their heads are firmly wedged in the clouds. It will be interesting to see what happens when those ladders turn into snakes.

**Eleanor Lang** (*Con*) made a cool £1 million profit when she sold two adjacent flats that she had acquired in Westminster for £1.8 million, having knocked them together into one property. Although the taxpayer had contributed £87,000 to the original purchase, Ms. Lang herself was rather less generous when it came to paying Capital Gains Tax on the proceeds of the sale and she appears satisfied that she does not have to share a penny of the £180,000 due with the tax authorities. If Party leaders order her to cough up the full amount, it will be the biggest repayment yet from any MP.

**Barry Gardiner** (*Lab*) has calculated that the profit he made on his Pimlico second home is all for the public good, although he won't be donating any of that money himself. Mr. Gardiner bought the flat for £246,500 and sold it four years later at a profit of £198,500. "If you do your arithmetic you may well conclude that the public purse has actually benefited from my purchase of a property", he said, going on to explain that "this is because the amount returned to the Exchequer in Capital Gains Tax approximates to the total amounts claimed over the entire four-year period". Neat – although the Capital Gains Tax liability at today's rate would amount to some £40,000, a little shy of the £81,935 he reclaimed in second home expenses over the same four years.

Greg Barker (*Con*), a near neighbour to Mr. Gardiner, bought a property in Pimlico for £480,000 in 2004, against which he claimed back nearly £16,000 in stamp duty and fees and £27,928 in mortgage interest payments. Two years later he sold it, pocketing a £320,000 profit, before flipping his second home to a flat he already owned just a few minutes' travel away in Chelsea.

Lynne Jones (*Lab*) made around £285,000 profit on her London second home, once she had lavished £22,000 of taxpayers' money on it. The socialist MP was candid about her good fortune, saying: "I have never made a secret of the fact I will make a profit on the property, as everyone who buys a home tends to do". Political principles to the fore, she did however concede that: "I would support clawing some of the money back for the taxpayer". We look forward to receiving it.

### Tony's Towers

Just how did a musically-inclined family man amass a property empire valued today at around £10 million? As newlyweds in 1980, the aspiring MP **Tony Blair** and his lawyer wife Cherie started off modestly enough with a terrace house in Dalston, East London, which they bought for £40,000. Three years later, having been elected as an MP, Mr. Blair acquired a house in his Sedgefield constituency, for which he took out a £30,000 mortgage. He remortgaged it twice, first for around £90,000 the same year to cover renovations and improvements (permitted under *The Green Book* guidelines) and then again at the end of 2003, when he took out a loan for £260,000. Meanwhile, the couple were making good progress in London. In 1986, having sold the Dalston house at a 100% profit, the Blairs relocated to a £120,000 house in Highbury where they remained until 1993, when they swapped the property for a grander address at 1 Richmond Crescent, Islington, paying £375,000. In 1997, however, they fell off the ladder with a bump, selling a property that would have grown to around £1.8 million over the next ten years for £615,000 after police informed them that the cost of installing security would be prohibitive. After settling into

Downing Street and the Prime Minister's official country retreat, Chequers, in 2002, Cherie ventured into the property market once more with the ill-advised purchase of a pair of flats in Bristol at £525,000, for which she engaged the negotiation services of the convicted Australian conman, Peter Foster, boyfriend of her mystic friend Carol Caplin. The couple's next acquisition, in 2004, was a large property in London's Connaught Square, for which they put down a deposit of £182,500 and secured a mortgage of £3,467,500 – more than 18 times Mr Blair's salary. Mind you, it was a safe enough bet, what with the lucrative promises of a prime-ministerial autobiography and innumerable post-partum public-speaking engagements. On leaving office three years later, the Blairs snapped up an adjoining mews house for a further £800,000 to create a stunning complex in the heart of London. Their total loan at this stage was been estimated at a whopping £4.45 million, which translates to around £18,500 a month on a 5% interest-only basis. They subsequently acquired a sixth property for £4 million: a 'small stately home' just a few miles from Chequers which "ticked all of Cherie's boxes".

*"But surely if this became our second home, we could do it up and double its size while we remortgage our fourth home and let the first".*

# WHICH PARTY...?

**Generally speaking, the dodgy expense claims followed party lines: property scams and low-brow/bling (sparkly loo seats) – Labour; property scams and reckless indulgence (moat cleaning) – Conservative; property scams and rather predictable (health products) – Liberal Democrats.**

Can you guess the parties of the MPs who made the following claims?

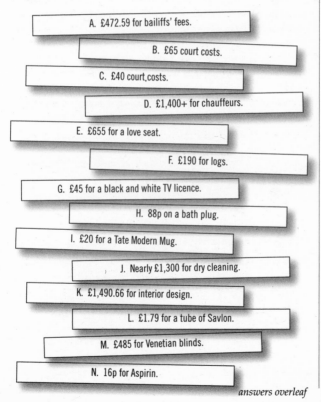

A. £472.59 for bailiffs' fees.

B. £65 court costs.

C. £40 court costs.

D. £1,400+ for chauffeurs.

E. £655 for a love seat.

F. £190 for logs.

G. £45 for a black and white TV licence.

H. 88p on a bath plug.

I. £20 for a Tate Modern Mug.

J. Nearly £1,300 for dry cleaning.

K. £1,490.66 for interior design.

L. £1.79 for a tube of Savlon.

M. £485 for Venetian blinds.

N. 16p for Aspirin.

*answers overleaf*

# ANSWERS - WHICH PARTY...?

A. *Labour* – **Sir Peter Soulsby** claimed back bailiffs' fees when the rent on his constituency office fell into arrears.

B. *Labour* – Perhaps a tad unjustly, former Junior Justice Minister **Shahid Malik** was able to claw back £65 for a summons issued after he failed to pay council tax.

C. *Liberal Democrats* – **Lembit Opik** was also reimbursed by the taxpayer for a court summons for forgetting to pay his council tax.

D. *Labour* - **Michael Martin** spent over £1,400 on chauffeurs in his Glasgow constituency during 2004-05.

E. *Conservative* – Anti-sleaze campaigner **Douglas Carswell**'s romantic purchase had a happy outcome. "I bought the love seat when moving to the home with my future wife. We have since got married and had our first baby". Ahhh!

F. *Conservative* – **James Gray** clearly reckons you can't beat a (free) real log fire.

G. *Labour* – **Chris Mullin**'s low-tech viewing habits should serve as an inspiration to some of his colleagues. "It may not be widescreen or high-definition or have Dolby SurroundSound and the like, but it still works fine enough for me", he explained.

H. *Labour* – When ex-Home Secretary **Jacqui Smith** bought this economical item, only her bath water was going down the plughole.

I. *Conservative* – The price **Michael Gove** paid for a single hot beverage receptacle raises the question of which one was the mug.

J. *Conservative* – **David Lidington** likes to be spick and span.

K. *Liberal Democrats* – **Menzies Campbell** agreed to pay back the money.

L. *Liberal Democrats* – **Martin Horwood** is the man who bought the soothing ointment.

M. *Sinn Fein* – The flat concerned is shared by five Sinn Fein MPs. It is one of three London properties rented and claimed for by the party, even though its elected representatives have not taken up their Parliamentary seats.

N. *Labour* – **Austin Mitchell** negotiated this striking bargain, perhaps after having over-indulged on ginger crinkle biscuits and Branston Pickle.

# HOW MUCH TAXPAYERS' MONEY DOES IT TAKE TO CHANGE A LIGHTBULB?

**The answer hinges on whether the MP is prepared to risk life and limb.**

**Keith Simpson** (*Con*), an ex-Sandhurst action man, appears to have seized the bull by the horns and performed this tricky task himself. As a result, the 60 halogen bulbs he had invoiced the taxpayer for since 2004 have worked out at a puny £3.10 a piece. **David** 'Two Brains' **Willetts** (*Con*) is a less reckless soul. Recognizing the limitations of his own practical abilities, the Shadow Secretary for Innovation, Universities and Skills got workmen to do the job for him. They charged £135 to replace 25 light bulbs at his West London pad, or £5.40 a throw.

### ... or Keep Your Chimneys in Order
**Barbara Follett**, the Labour Member for Stevenage, submitted a claim for £384 for sweeping the eight chimneys atop her four-storey second home town-house in Soho. Doesn't the Culture Secretary know she's living in a smokeless zone? Don't panic though, she only has gas fires in the grate. According to her constituency-based sooty, the chimneys must nevertheless be annually checked (for what?) to keep in line with "rules and regulations". He also sweeps her flues at the Minister's main home in Hertfordshire, which only boasts a modest six chimneys.

### ... or Impress the Girls
Cheeky chappy **Lembit Opik** (*LibDem*), best known for his relationships with weather-girl Sian Lloyd and Romanian *chanteuse* Gabriela Irimia, submitted a rather barefaced expenses claim after spending £2,499 on a plasma screen telly in 2005. It was refused in part because the playboy wasn't actually an MP at the time, Parliament having been dissolved ahead of that year's General Election.

"I've ironed the Telegraph for you, sir."

"Oh why don't you piss off back to your quarters Jones, and take that ghastly rag with you"

# BEYOND PROPRIETY?

The Additional Cost Allowance (ACA) for 'second home' property claims was inevitably the most attractive, but not the only, temptation available to Britain's MPs. There were considerable additional claimable allowances available (and open to abuse), not least office and staff expenses, of which many took full advantage.

## Taxing Questions

The fact that most MPs are 'self-employed', and therefore are not registered as 'Pay-As-You-Earn' (PAYE), means that they have to submit 'Self Assessment' tax returns. This suggests that there might have been considerable leeway for elasticizing, if not bending, the rules. While claiming tax advice on expenses claims is reclaimable, getting your entire Self-Assessment form sorted out by an accountant isn't (although these costs are claimable against your personal annual business running costs according to the Inland Revenue). Confused? Not as much as several MPs including, notably, Chancellor of the Exchequer **Alistair Darling** and playmate **Geoff Hoon**, among several others.

## Recurring Patterns

An interesting obsession with clearing MPs' properties of bugs and pests (including moles) emerged as a frequent pattern, as did a tendency to employ unlikely members of their own families as 'office staff'. In 2008, it emerged that **Peter Hain** (*Lab*) was touchingly supplementing her pension by employing his 80-year old mother Adelaine as a part-time secretary on a salary of £5,400 per annum. Indeed she had been working in this capacity – reportedly very hard – since 1991. In her (previous) day, the undoubtedly very able South Africa-born Mrs. Hain was a prominent anti-apartheid activist. Whether it was she who might have forgotten to mention the £103,000 donation to her son's Socialist party election effort, which Mr. Hain in turn forgot to disclose to the House of Commons committee (see Disclosure) remains a matter for conjecture.

# SNOUTS IN THE TROUGH

Never mind going to work on an egg. Without having to set foot outside the Palace of Westminster, MPs can stuff themselves at a plethora of bars, cafés, brasseries and restaurants, all operated by the Refreshment Department. These eateries are all heavily subsidized by the taxpayer – to the tune of £4.8 million in 2006-07 – so even the piggiest of our parliamentary representatives should find it a challenge to chomp his or her way through their £4,800 annual food allowance. Some of them have given it a fair go though:

**Graham Stuart** (*Con*) guzzled his way through an impressive £8,400 worth of food over just three years, including £2,000 in each of 2005 and 2008, and a whopping £4,400 in 2006-07 when he presumably fell off his diet for a few months.

**Michael Moore** (*Lib Dem*) is a fan of home cooking, and apparently doesn't like to stint on quality ingredients. In just one year he managed to clock up £3,100 on food at his London flat.

**John Hemming** (*Lib Dem*) claimed the maximum amount allowable for food throughout both 2006-07 and 2007-08, mostly in House of Commons restaurants and canteens – even when the Commons was not sitting. And still that wasn't enough. On his blog, Mr. Hemming confessed: "I spend a lot more than this sum of money on eating during the year", going on to point out that he pays workers in one of his companies a more than generous £50 a day just for food. That's a lot of sandwiches.

Some MPs like to indulge in a little snacking between meals to keep their energy levels up. **Charles Kennedy** (*Lib Dem*) went on a bit of a binge when he bought three boxes of mints

The Little Book of Big Expenses

*"Hang on a minute! That still leaves £1.22 on the full annual allowance. Clear these plates and fetch me a menu!"*

from the House of Commons gift shop, perhaps offering one to **Andrew Rosindell** (*Con*) to remove any traces of fishy breath after his £1.31 tub of jellied eels.

**Derek Wyatt** (*Lab*) has a weakness for meaty nibbles, claiming 75p for two Scotch eggs, £1.75 for five mini pork pies and a further £1.90 for an individual pork pie. The greatest grazer of them all, however, must surely be Shadow Minister for Europe **Mark Francois**, whose expense receipts listed delicacies ranging from Kit Kats, Mars bars and ice cream to Peperami, Pringle crisps, Twiglets and Pot Noodles. A former soldier who lists hill walking as one of his hobbies, Mr. Francois is well aware that eating so many sweeties can be bad for dental health. His expenses also included £12.94 for toothbrushes.

In addition to invoicing the Fees Office for ginger crinkle biscuits and Branston Pickle, **Austin Mitchell** (*Lab*) has also pocketed 16p for lemons and charged bottles of wine and spirits to the taxpayer. Some of these claims appear to have surprised even him. "Money spent on ginger crinkles and Branston Pickle shocks me", he announced. "Neither is made in Grimsby [his constituency] but I am instituting immediate enquires in my household to see who could possibly be responsible for introducing such dangerous substances. I have not so far traced empty containers of either. Whisky and gin are another matter. I drink neither. I will check to see if my wife is an alcoholic and take appropriate action".

**Andrew Turner** (*Con*) was also more interested in liquid sustenance. As his parliamentary secretary (and girlfriend) explained to the Fees Office, she was particularly looking forward to using his refunded office expenses to buy "lots of booze" which, she hoped, would help the 2005 election slip by in an "alcoholic blur".

# THE LAP OF LUXURY

Distinguishing between what might be seen as a practical need and what can only be seen as excessive indulgence is a problem which many MPs addressed quite conscientiously. Some, however, certainly pushed the envelope far too far. For example, when MPs were redecorating a second home, or a home that might soon be 'flipped', the specialist paint producers Farrow & Ball seem to have made a substantial turnover at the taxpayer's expense. Why? You can get the same colours mixed down the road at B&Q for a fraction of the price. And so often it was the claimants from the upper echelons of society (and by no means all of them were Tories) who failed to comprehend that we are now meant to be living in Mr. Blair's 'classless' civil society.

## In Darkest Soho

In addition to her gleaming collection of chimneys noted elsewhere, the Minister for Culture, Creative Industries and Tourism, and MP for sunny Stevenage, **Barbara Follett** handed in some industrially creative expense claims. Being married to millionaire popular novelist Ken Follett probably qualified her for the 'Culture' part of her official moniker as much as her attributed invention of Labour's 'red rose' logo. Around the time of her election Ken and Barbie forsook their luxury home near Cheyne Walk for a country house in her Hertfordshire constituency, and a four-storey 'pied-à-terre' in Soho. Noted for her 'champagne socialist' lifestyle, Ms. Follett does not admittedly claim mortgage interest for a second home, but soaks up the taxpayer's money in other ways, viz. her claim for £25,400-worth of private 'security services' when scuttling home to London's notorious vice-ridden square mile, but also £937 in 'fine art' insurance, £528.75 for antique rug refurbishment (deemed excessive, but she still copped £228.75 reimbursement) and a further £600 a year for Rentokil to check for pests.

# IT'S THE THOUGHT THAT COUNTS

Scots have been serving in the UK's armed forces for hundreds of years. Over 148,000 of them died in the First World War alone. Today, there are some 25,000 Scots in receipt of a war pension for services to their country. When Remembrance Day comes around each November, Scottish MPs are quick to mark their respect by laying a poppy wreath in honour of their fallen compatriots. Unfortunately, 15 of them – from the SNP, Labour and the Lib Dems – have been equally speedy in reclaiming the cost on expenses, as permitted under Scottish Parliament rules.* They have since been shamed into repaying every last penny.

**Frank Cook**, Labour MP for Stockton North, tried to claim back the cost of giving £5 to a church collection at a Battle of Britain memorial service. The Fees Office felt that Mr. Cook might like to reconsider, and rejected the claim. A repentant Mr. Cook told Sky News: "I don't know how it happened, it is wrong that it happened, I can't explain it and I am sorry that it has happened. I can't give any better explanation because I don't have one. I am not going to turn round and blame some member of staff. I am responsible. That's it. I can't explain it. I'm sorry".

Anyone who considers the Scots mean is, of course, subscribing to an ancient cliché with no real foundation. But **Bill Butler**, Labour MSP for Glasgow Anniesland, didn't exactly help dispel the myth when he tried to claw back a £1 donation to charity that was made by a hotel in his name. The Scottish Parliament authorities duly rejected the claim. He subsequently maintained that the donation was made without his knowledge. That's alright then.

Oh dear, oh dear, another MSP letting the national side down. When **Alex Fergusson** (Presiding Officer of the Scottish

Parliament) took out an advert to congratulate a charity for disadvantaged children in his constituency, hearts were no doubt warmed. Until, that is, he tried to reclaim £132.78 for the cost. The claim was rejected.

Christmas is a time to remember old friends and those less fortunate than ourselves. Like many of us, **David Whitton**, MSP for Strathkelvin and Bearsden, likes to do his bit for seasonal goodwill by sending out a flurry of Christmas cards. Unfortunately, he doesn't like paying for them. The Scottish Parliament authorities fingered him as a bit of a Scrooge and rejected his claim for £290 for printing costs.

Unlike their Scottish counterparts, MPs south of the border have been prohibited from reclaiming the cost of charitable items since 2004. Plainly, a few of them are unaware that Remembrance Day wreaths aren't just pretty, if artificial, flower arrangements. **Boris Johnson** (*Con*), **James Gray** (*Con*), **Ed Balls** (*Lab*), **Tom Levitt** (*Lab*) and **Brian Gibbons** (*Lab*) have all reportedly tried to claim for the poppies since the practice was outlawed.

After purchasing three boxes of mints and two toffee-coloured teddy bears from the Commons gift shop, **Charles Kennedy** (*Lib Dem*) donated them to a charity prize draw. This heart-warming gesture was rather spoiled when he claimed back the £35.75 as Incidental Expenses. "I receive regular requests for fundraising and other charitable causes", Mr Kennedy explained. "These I meet from my own pocket and am happy to do so". The claims were repaid on 11th May, once the expenses scandal was in full flow.

*It is noteworthy that MSPs are scarcely to be found on other pages of this book. The Scottish parliament has a far more transparent expenses system than the equivalent at Westminster. MSPs' expense claims are published in exquisite detail every three months. Lest the good folk of Holyrood should be tempted to get on a moral high horse, we should point out the system was only adopted after a furore in the Scottish press. Mind you, there's probably little left in the petty cash box after the cost of the new Parliament building escalated tenfold from an original provision of £40 million to £431 million.

# GREEN BENCHES

Who'd have known there were so many green fingers in the House of Commons? An MP's (second) home may be his castle, but his garden is where his heart is. Clearly preferring 'Gardeners' Question Time' to the indoor tedium of 'Prime Minister's Questions', MPs have claimed thousands for all manner of horticultural paraphernalia, from horse manure to red cedars and duck houses. And with a good few MPs going on imminent 'gardening leave', Alan Titchmarsh should watch his back.

**Christopher Fraser** (*Con*) loves his pigs. But you can be sure he doesn't let them anywhere near his prize blooms. In fact, in 2007 he installed £875 worth of fencing at taxpayers' expense to ensure that his garden's boundaries were clearly defined and any undesirables kept out: "There were occasions when I found people and dogs in the garden" he complained. Whatever next? At the same time he claimed a further £933 for trees, including 140 cherry laurels and 75 red cedars. Perhaps he wanted to give the pigs their own wood to roam in. When it came to keeping the lawn in order, he claimed £240 for "the cheapest lawnmower that I could find" and thoughtfully saved the public purse even more money when he "cut the grass myself to save costs".

**Anthony Steen** (*Con*) has more trees than he knows quite what to do with, although the rabbits on his sprawling estate are trying their best to relieve him of the problem. The public cost of maintaining his £1 million house and grounds in Devon over a period of four years amounted to a dizzying £87,729. Among the individual items claimed for was the sum of £459 for a woodland consultant to come and look at new trees and give advice on 'additional guarding' against rabbits. Another forest expert was called out to survey the laurels and rhododendrons and inspect some 500 trees. Justifying the work, Mr. Steen pointed out that at least part of it was necessitated by the safety concerns of his whingeing constituents. Mystified by "all the fuss" and saddened that his almost royal residence has inspired only jealousy among voters, Mr. Steen then decided to spend more time with his beloved trees.

**David Heathcoat-Amory**'s (*Con*) garden must be a wonder to behold. As well as the infamous 19 separate claims for a staggering 550+ bags of horse manure (works wonders on roses), his costs have ranged from a few pounds to thousands. Here are some of the smaller ones:

> **Seeds: £1.95** on sunflower seeds, for planting not eating.

> **Mouse poison: £2**. Presumably to keep the blighters off the sunflower seeds.

> **Wheelbarrow puncture: £5**. Essential for shifting all that manure.

> **Hedge-trimming: £30.** Keeps the orchard hedge tidy.

> **Lawn maintenance: over £50** for herbicide, moss-killer and weed-and-feed.

Not that he can take the credit for doing all the work himself. Larger claims include:

> **£605.25** for 67.5 hours of 'gardening services' in 2005.

> **£1,792.50** for payments to a gardening business in 2007.

> **£2,371.86** for further payments to the same company in 2008.

It's a wonder the Fees Office didn't send round a bulldozer.

**Sir Peter Viggers** (*Con*) is another MP who has great faith in the beneficial properties of manure – to such an extent that he ordered 28 tons of the stuff, a bargain at £500. He didn't stop there, however, managing to clock up around £30,000 on gardening expenses overall. With every inch of the place having been done over – he even had his initials emblazoned in gold on a well cover – it was only a matter of time before the inadequacies of his duck pond came to his attention.

Scandinavian home decor being in vogue, he ordered a £1,645 32-square foot floating 'Stockholm' duck house to keep the birds safe from marauding foxes, who were no doubt dumbfounded by the spectacle. Sadly, the ducks were not impressed and the house was relocated to Sir Peter's *château* in France, presumably on the basis that French ducks have better taste. The Fees Office was not impressed either and queried the cost. Sir Peter has since said that he bought the item himself. A new 'second home' perhaps?

**Douglas Hogg** (*Con*) is famous for having the cleanest moat in the country– at £2,000, there shouldn't be so much as a water-snail in sight. But the beautification of his garden did not stop there. Having shelled out – and reclaimed – £6,800 on a gardener for an eight-month period in 2003 and a further £1,000 for having the lawn mown (curiously not one of the gardener's duties), Mr. Hogg was damned if a load of moles were going to set up home on his property. Accordingly, he spent £247 addressing the problem. Following a certain furore over the moat claim, Mr. Hogg has announced that he will soon be raising the drawbridge and retiring to fight the moles alone.

**David Cameron** (*Con*) bucked the party trend by being rather more interested in checking nature's ambition than encouraging it. In November 2006, forsaking the Whip in favour of a professional contractor, he claimed £680 for work on his second home, which included the cost of stripping back an unruly wisteria and removing another troublesome vine from his chimney.

**Michael Howard** (*Con*), survivor of a 12-round hammering by Jeremy Paxman, may throw in the trowel after it was revealed that he lavished over £17,000 on the garden of his constituency property near Folkestone between 2004 and 2008. Appropriately enough, one of the companies that he employed to tend his precious sward rejoiced in the name of 'The Turned Worm'. Mr. Howard denied that all of the invoices were for gardening services alone, stating that the company undertook

*"Do you think the taxpayer will stand it?"*

*" Of course – it's a bloody eyesore. You're better off with some leylandii to keep the rabble at bay."*

domestic maintenance work as well. The Turned Worm's owner, a Mr. Steve Hare, seemed more than a little confused about the matter when he explained: "If a drain needs unblocking, there is painting or a tree has come down, then they will call me to clear a tree from the drive".

Some MPs have full-time gardeners on their payroll, though not necessarily at their expense. **Sir John Butterfill** (*Con*) used his expense account to build an entire new wing on his second home in Woking to house the gardener and his wife. However, the Tory grandee's use of nomenclature raised questions about whether this employee's duties were restricted to horticulture. When he went on BBC's Newsnight to explain his £17,000 claim, Sir John described the Telegraph's allegation that he had described the extension as "servants' quarters" as "a gross misrepresentation". A few sentences later he grossly misrepresented himself. "The mistake I made", he explained, "was that, in claiming interest [from the expenses allowance] on the home, I didn't separate from that the value of the servants' … er … the staff … wing."

# DOWN THE PAN

MPs' views on the monarchy often make the news, but you can learn a lot about them – perhaps more than you need to know – by studying their attitudes to that 'other' kind of throne:

**John Reid** *(Lab)* – When it comes to loo seats, most of us would have the former Home Secretary down as an unpainted pine man. In fact, an expense claim reveals that he prefers a glittery black number.

**John Prescott** *(Lab)* – 'Two Jags' ran the risk of being renamed 'Two Loo Seats' after invoicing the Fees Office for repairs to broken items of that nature in December 2004 and September 2006.

**Peter Luff** *(Con)* – The champion lavatory seat claimant outdid John Prescott by getting the taxpayer to cough up for three seats in the space of two years. Perhaps this was related to overuse of the three kettles he purchased during the same period. Maybe he was just taking the piss.

**Mark Hoban** *(Con)* – The Fareham MP was flushed out when he charged the taxpayer £35 for a loo-roll holder and £18 for a toilet brush, useful items when doing parliamentary business.

**Christine Russell** *(Lab)* – Ms. Russell got £60 from the Fees Office in 2007 for the replacement of a broken loo seat. "I have never claimed for anything that is considered to be personal", she remarked controversially.

**Derek Conway** *(Con)* – Unlike Sir Peter Viggers, Mr Conway's waterfowl-related claim seems positively reasonable. The Fees Office awarded him 83p for a Toilet Duck.

**Gordon Brown** *(Lab)* – 'Wee' Gordon was reimbursed to the tune of £88.13 for getting the plumbers in to unblock a loo in his Fife home in 2007. Looks like he negotiated prudent good value for the average emergency call-out fee.

# I THOUGHT YOU'D NEVER ASK!

Can you match the MP to the item and its cost, below? For 2 bonus points, can you identify which items were rejected by the Fees Office?

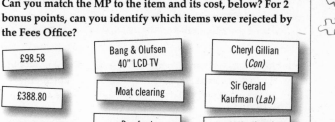

| Cost | Item | MP |
|---|---|---|
| £98.58 | Bang & Olufsen 40" LCD TV | Cheryl Gillian (*Con*) |
| £388.80 | Moat clearing | Sir Gerald Kaufman (*Lab*) |
| £8,865 | Dog food | David Heathcoat-Amory (*Con*) |
| £185.89 | Horse manure | Quentin Davies (*Lab*) |
| £10,033.33 | 60 halogen lightbulbs | Sir Gerald Kaufman (*Lab*) |
| £1,100 | Second-hand rug | Patrick McLoughlin (*Con*) |
| £1,645 | Removal of wasps' nest | Keith Simpson (*Con*) |
| £135.12 | Window frames | Lynn Jones (*Lab*) |
| £4.47 | Floating duck house | Douglas Hogg (*Con*) |
| £2,200 | Replacing 25 lightbulbs | David Willetts (*Con*) |
| £1,461.83 | Swimming pool heater | Michael Ancram (*Con*) |
| £158.63 | Wallpaper | Sir Peter Viggers (*Con*) |

*answers overleaf*

# ANSWERS

| Amount | Item | Beneficiary |
|---|---|---|
| £158.63 | Removal of wasps' nest | Patrick McLoughlin |
| £8,865 | Bang & Olufsen 40" LCD TV | Sir Gerald Kaufman |
| £1,461.83 | Second-hand rug (plus £398.91 customs for importing it from the US) | Sir Gerald Kaufman |
| £388.80 | Horse manure | David Heathcoat-Amory |
| £135.12 | Replacing 25 lightbulbs | David Willetts |
| £2,200 | Moat clearing | Douglas Hogg |
| £98.58 | Swimming pool heater repair | Michael Ancram |
| £4.47 | Dog food | Cheryl Gillian |
| £10,033.33 | Window frames | Quentin Davies |
| £185.89 | 60 halogen lightbulbs | Keith Simpson |
| £1,645 | Floating duck house | Sir Peter Viggers |
| £1,100 | Wallpaper | Lynne Jones |

Items NOT (fully) paid for by the taxpayer:

**Removal of wasps' nest:** rejected on the grounds that the claim was made for his home address.

**Bang & Olufsen TV**: maximum amount allowed for a TV is £750.

**Duck house**: this was queried (unsurprisingly) by the Fees Office. Although Sir Peter Viggers claimed a massive £30,000 against gardening expenses, he has since maintained that he treated the ducks to their palatial new accommodation himself.

# BUT...

It's not all bad news: some of our MPs, clearly feeling pricked by their consciences, fell over themselves to make amends. **Sir Peter Viggers** agreed to pay back a whopping £10,000 of 'excessive' garden expenses. **Michael Ancram** wrote a letter to his constituents apologizing wholeheartedly for the oversight of charging them to repair his pool boiler. We're getting the cost of clearing that moat back too. **David Willetts** agreed to refund the taxpayer in full for the cost of changing his light bulbs. And the dog food? **Cheryl Gillian**, not to be outdone in this new spirit of generosity, refunded every penny of the £4.47.

**Quentin Davies** (*Lab*) however remained unrepentant. Of the cost of maintaining his 18th-century listed second home, he said: "I choose to live in a house in Lincolnshire, the upkeep and maintenance of which certainly costs considerably more than the total allowance available under the ACA, and always has and will. I make no complaint about that – it is simply a personal choice".\* His main home is a flat in London.

**Anthony Steen** (*Con*) is also unrepentant. After claiming nearly £90,000 over four years he suggested people were "jealous" of his Balmoral-style large second home. Mr Steen described his behaviour as "impeccable" and said he had merely been "caught on the wrong foot".

\* 'Choice' is obviously a subject close to this minister's heart. Take the matter of exactly which party to support: having been a Tory MP for 20 years, Davies had a change of heart and defected from the Conservatives to join the Labour party the very night before Gordon Brown became Prime Minister. Just two years earlier he had said of his future boss, the then Chancellor: "I trust and believe that something nasty will happen to the Chancellor in electoral terms before too long. He will have no one but himself to blame".

\*\*On 2nd June, to add to the Labour Party's escalating travails, it was announced that some £32 million was needed from the public purse to shore up the crumbling edifices occupied by the Royal Family. A sneakily prescient piece of manoeuvring then by the Hon. Member for Totnes.

# NEVER KNOWINGLY UNDERCLAIMED

The names 'John Lewis' and 'Peter Jones' are music to many a middle-class ear. Over the years, generations of wedding list compilers and, it turns out, MPs have beaten a path to the Oxford Street emporium and her sister store in upmarket Sloane Square. So popular, in fact, were the stores for kitting out MPs' second homes that the official *Additional Costs Claims Guide* was known as the 'John Lewis List'.

For a long time, the Guide was successfully kept from the prying eyes of the general public; in 2008, when quizzed about its existence by journalists, the then Director-General of Resources at the Fees Office only added to the mystery when he responded: "It doesn't exist in paper form and whether it can be printed, I don't know". When details were eventually published later that year there was public outcry at the scale of allowances, such as £10,000 for a kitchen and over £6,000 for a new bathroom. In response, the Government placed a cap on expenditure on household items at 10% of the maximum second homes allowance of £24,000. Dubbed the 'Ikea List', this compromise persisted until May 2009 when, after further outrage from taxpayers, MPs were no longer allowed to claim at all for furniture or household goods.

So, John Lewis or Ikea? Who shops where?

### John Lewis/Peter Jones
Frequented by members of all parties, the stores catered for a wide range of tastes and budgets, and it seems our MPs couldn't quite resist picking out the odd item from the pricier end of the spectrum. When Lib Dem MP **Richard Younger-Ross** treated himself to a £1,475 designer chest-of-drawers in cherry wood plus £725 matching mirror his party leaders suggested he might have gone a bit far. Complaining that

"When you go into Parliament, nobody tells you what 'luxury' is", Mr. Younger-Ross has agreed to refund the taxpayer.

Tory **Tim Yeo**, always a colourful character, had a sense of humour failure when news of his purchase of a £906 laptop in a fetching shade of pink raised a few titters. "A laptop is a laptop whatever colour it is and this is a trivial point", he snapped. Labour MP **Michael Connarty**'s purchase of a £228.95 alarm clock must surely have been a wake-up call for the Fees Office (curiously, he also claimed £249.99 for an alarm clock acquired at Comet within the same two-year period).

**Keith Vaz** (*Lab*), though, wins the prize for seeking out the most luxurious products, managing to spend over £480 at John Lewis on 22 cushions, most of them silk, and lavishing a further £2,614 on a pair of leather armchairs with matching footstool.

### Ikea

The Swedish furnishing emporium is a magnet to Labour MPs. When staying at his second home **Alistair Darling** relaxes on a *chaise longue* he purchased there; Andy Burnham is known to have a penchant for Ikea bathrobes (unlike the Fees Office, who rejected that one) and the pride of **Peter Soulsby**'s dining room is his £155 Ikea sideboard.

One nameless MP charged the public purse 5p for an Ikea carrier bag (happily reusable). Understandably, said MP wishes to keep his or her identity shielded from the guffaws of the paying public. All we know for sure is that he or she was a member of the Labour party with a constituency in Scotland. A little investigation quickly reveals that there are just two Ikea stores in Scotland, both of which fall within Labour constituencies – those of **David Hamilton** and **Jim Sheridan** respectively.

So, just for fun and without in any way pointing fingers (there are plenty of Labour MPs north of the border), which of the two is the more likely to have needed an Ikea bag?

**Jim Sheridan**, MP for Paisley & Renfrewshire North, is a man of expensive tastes – at least where the taxpayer is footing the bill. For his second home in London he claimed a hefty £991.95 for a luxurious 'ivory leather bed' and a further £699.99 for a plasma TV. A tad pricey for Ikea, perhaps. That's not to say such a big spender would necessarily stop short of picking up a bargain or two at the superstore when he pops up to his constituency.

**Mr. Hamilton**, the Midlothian MP, on the other hand, claimed for rather less lavish items for his London pad – although £200 for bedding and £165 on mirrors still sounds a bit steep for the Scandinavian superstore. Perhaps there is a further clue to whether he has ever visited the shop. His website displays a fetching photo of Mr Hamilton, flanked by a pair of Scottish lovelies, at a coffee morning in support of the cancer charity Macmillan. The venue for this worth event was none other than... Ikea. One hopes he donated generously to the campaign from his own pocket.

Ikea kitchens are coveted for their sleek designs and nifty storage solutions, and it seems Labour MPs can't get enough of them. Top of the range was **Gordon Brown**'s £9,000 refit in 2005, costly enough for him to have to spread the claim over two years. The following year, Calder Valley MP **Chris McCafferty** took a leaf out of her leader's book when she decked her second home out with a somewhat cheaper model at £2,000. **Phil Hope**, MP for Corby and East Northants, plumped for a mid-range kitchen which he proceeded to fill with equipment ranging from a set of saucepans at £240 to £235 for wall and floor tiles.

The Lib Dems are not averse to a spot of bargain-hunting at Ikea either, although **Nick Clegg** hardly went wild on his last visit, spending a mere £4.99 on cushions, £2.49 on a cake pan and £1.50 on paper napkins. Mr. Clegg has however also confessed to having an Ocado habit. Ocado is the online delivery service for the supermarket Waitrose, which is of course owned by John Lewis.

"I found some dear little fingerbowls at Peter Jones today, and realized we hadn't got any. I ordered a couple of dozen in case we are entertaining".

# KEEPING IT IN THE FAMILY

In 2008, the European Parliament declared that British MEPs would no longer be able to employ family members on grounds that the system is too open to fraud (*see* Our Colleagues Over There). This was after Euro auditors discovered that around 80% of the £106 million spent on salaries for MEPs' assistants was not supported by sufficient proof of any actual work being done. UK MEPs employ more family members than any other European parliament member. Westminster has yet to follow suit with its own nepotism ban: in May 2009 more than 200 MPs were employing relatives at a total estimated cost, according to *The Daily Telegraph*, to the taxpayer of up to £5.8 million per year.

### The Thicker-Than-Water Trophy

Here are just a few who have been known to keep it in the family:

### First Prize

**Derek Conway** , the former Conservative Whip, paid his sons Henry and Freddie a total of £85,000 to do 'research' for him. This was perhaps not unconnected with the fact that Henry, who has described himself as "blond, bouncy and one of the boys", decided to throw a little do at a Chelsea nightclub entitled 'The Fuck Off I'm Rich Party'. Freddie, for his part, was described in a Commons report as having been "almost invisible" in Westminster during the period he was supposedly working for his Dad. "Nonsense!" cried Conway, reaching for an unfortunately Freudian metaphor: "He would go up and down [from Newcastle, where he was a full-time student] like a fiddler's elbow". The Commons suspended Conway for ten days in January 2008; the Tories kicked him out of the party.

The Little Book of Big Expenses

*"Daddy, what are you going to pay me to do tomorrow?"*

## Runner-Up

**Julie Kirkbride** (*Con*) pays her sister Karen Leadley £12,000 to answer letters from her constituents in Worcestershire. Slightly embarrassingly, Karen lives more than 100 miles away in Dorset. The Bromsgrove MP also got her brother to buy around £1,000-worth of electrical equipment on the internet. Naturally, "they were entirely related to my parliamentary duties".

## Honourable Mentions

Once noted radical socialist **Glenda Jackson** (*Lab*) employs her niece as a parliamentary intern at her Hampstead and Highgate constituency office. In the interests of fairness, we should add that the star of *Women in Love* doesn't claim travel expenses as she makes good use of her London Freedom Pass.

The leader of the Democratic Unionist Party **Peter Robinson** and his wife **Iris** (also *DUP*) are well known for their endorsement of family values. They certainly get good value out of their family and vice-versa. All three of their children – Jonathan, Gareth and Rebekah – are employed on their staff, plus a daughter-in-law for good measure.

Bicycling baronet **Sir George Young** (*Con*) employs his daughter Camilla as his office manager. He also happens to be chairman of the Commons Standards and Privileges Committee.

### The Other Half

From August 2008, all MPs were made to declare family members in their employ. The results were staggering, with more than a quarter of all MPs across the parties claiming staffing allowance costs for their dearest, if not nearest. The vast majority of family members employed are the wives of male MPs and it seems they are a multi-talented lot, working in various roles (in addition to sundry traditional conjugal duties) as diary secretaries, constituency secretaries, executive secretaries, personal assistants, parliamentary assistants, office managers, case-workers and researchers.

### Jobs for the Girls

These women must be applauded; their jobs involve working long and often anti-social hours, and how many of us would relish

*"Your mother's on the phone. She says the people from the Telegraph keep asking her what she does, exactly, as your Diary Secretary and she wants to know what she should tell them."*

taking orders – let alone dictation – day in, day out, from our other halves? As **Peter Luff** (*Con*) explained: "Few people understand the burdens involved in being a Member of Parliament's secretary. The work is more intense by far than any work I am aware of similar people in the private sector [doing]. The constant flow of telephone calls, the e-mails and letters as well as personal callers means there is always more work to be done". Clearly, nobody else would be up to the job. Here are just a few examples:

| MP | Wife | Job Title | Annual Salary |
|---|---|---|---|
| Nick Ainger (*Lab*) | Sally | Case-worker | £19,800 |
| Ian Austin (*Lab*) | Cathy | Parliamentary Asst | £8,000 |
| Sir Stuart Bell (*Lab*) | Margaret | Case-worker | £35,000 |
| Malcolm Bruce (*Lib Dem*) | Rosemary | Constituency Worker | £28,500 |
| Dr. Ian Gibson (*Lab*) | Liz | Diary Secretary | £10,000 |
| Stephen Hammond (*Con*) | Sally | Office Manager | £27,500 |
| Kelvin Hopkins (*Lab*) | Pat | Constituency Sec | £12,500 |
| Owen Paterson (*Con*) | Rose | Diary Secretary | £29,636 |
| Sir Peter Soulsby (*Lab*) | Alison | Secretary | £20,000 |

It is interesting that a Lib Dem constituency worker earns more than twice the salary of a Labour constituency secretary, while a Labour case-worker puts all of them (plus most of the country's average salaries) deeply in the shade.

## Tangled Webs

One MP who has employed successive partners in an official capacity is **James Gray** (*Con*). In 2007 Mr. Gray was claiming £2,400 a month for the services of his wife, Sarah, even though she had ceased to work as his secretary two years previously when she become ill with breast cancer. During this period Mr. Gray was having an affair with another woman, Philippa Mayo, whom he ultimately left his wife for – claiming a further £5,000 on expenses for the cost of moving in with his mistress – and who has since been installed as the MP's

Diary Secretary. Struggling to fit his political duties in with his complex personal life, at the time he appointed Ms Mayo, Mr Grey was also assisted by a full-time secretary in Westminster, a part-time secretary at his local association and a parliamentary researcher.

An altogether jollier story is that of **David Clelland** (*Con*), who is keen to point out that "I did not make my wife my secretary – I made my secretary my wife". Mr. Clelland employed Brenda Graham in 1985 on the recommendation of a friend and found her to be "bright and articulate" at interview. More of a steady breeze than a whirlwind romance, over the course of 20 years their "close relationship became a man and wife relationship" and the couple married in 2005. Ever-appreciative of his wife's many fine qualities, the Member for Tyne Bridge is happy for his wife to have retained her maiden name for work: "She did not want to be considered just 'the MP's wife' rather than the efficient and experienced secretary she had become".

### Honourable Mention

An honorary award goes to **Michael Clapham** (*Lab*), who touchingly dug into public funds to the tune of £210 to provide his wife, Yvonne, with a new pair of glasses. She also happens to work as his secretary.

### And for the Boys...

The Labour Member for Sheffield Heeley, **Meg Munn**, employs her husband Dennis Bates as a parliamentary assistant. Mr. Bates, who spent 12 years working for the Inland Revenue, also has an interesting sideline. In recent years he has received more than £5,000 for giving tax advice to five of his wife's colleagues, including David Miliband.

Graham Henderson, the husband of Shadow Minister for Health **Anne Milton**, was paid £13,000 for working for her as a researcher between 2005 and 2007. Mr. Henderson must have been a busy chap – he also spent the 2005/06 tax year employed as the Director of Public Health for the East Surrey Primary Care Trust.

# TO SPEND OR NOT TO SPEND?

It's a tricky question when there is so much on offer. Many MPs were quite conscientious in approaching the heaving table of possibilities on offer, but some were simply out for what they could get. And to a certain extent the self-importance which many of our elected lawmakers attach to themselves seems to have occasionally coloured their judgement.

### "Taxi, Please!"

Working-class hero and 'late-lamented' Speaker, **Michael Martin** fought a valiant four-year battle to prevent MPs' expenses (MPs on all sides of the House) from being disclosed. And what was his reward? Dismissal through disappointment. The poor man's personal claims had never been that excessive, but several of them display some aspirations towards clambering up the social ladder (albeit a tricky ascent for this uncharismatic figure). Why, for example, choose the brand 'Aristocrat' as your carpet replacement of choice for your constituency home? It's bound to raise an eyebrow. He attracted the most public criticism for his £1,400 claim for 12 chauffeur-driven saloon-car trips in his Glasgow North East constituency, which included visits to social housing projects, the Springburn Job Centre, the North Glasgow Housing Association, John Smith House (the HQ of the Scottish Labour Party) and to Celtic Park, home of Celtic Football Club. Despite his office claiming that "certain circumstances… require" that the Hon. Member be driven, and that using a government car would be more expensive, did no-one point out that constituents at many of these locations might prefer not to have their noses rubbed in it, at their expense?

# WHO DID THEY THINK THEY WERE KIDDING?

In addition to moat-cleaning, mole victimization, houses for your wildfowl collection etc., there were still a number of claims which prompted this critical question. Extraordinarily, the claimants in this category really didn't seem to think there was anything unusual – let alone wrong – with seeking compensation for spending their hard-earned cash.

### Splash!

**Michael Ancram** (*Con*) was not the only MP to assume that the taxpayer should pay for cleaning his swimming pool; **James Arbuthnot** (*Con*) prefers a dip in his country residence pool to a round of tennis (*see below*) after a hard day at the Defence Select Committee, so it's no surprise that he expected us taxpayers to foot the bill for cleaning it, and trimming the surrounding lawns, paying garden staff etc... Once he'd tired of his rented Hampshire mansion, in 2007 he somehow bought a £2 million residence – mortgage free!

### Deuce!

Meanwhile, across the country in Somerset **Oliver Letwin** (*Con*) deemed repairing a leaking pipe beneath the tennis court at his second home absolutely essential to his performance as an MP. He needs a bit of R&R after fulfilling his duties as a non-executive director at a City investment bank, membership of the Shadow Cabinet, chairmanship of the Conservative Research Department and of the party's Policy Review – where, interestingly, he is charged with sniffing out potential savings in the public sector. (For purposes of transparency, that's what the Government spends on the public – not what the public spend on the Government).

## Supermarket Sweep!

Lest it look as if we are finger-pointing rather too much at the Conservative contingent, here's a more desperate story from the opposite benches. As the winter months draw to a close, our thoughts turn to sprucing up our properties. Some MPs turn out to be even more prone than the rest of us to indulging in a little extra shopping at this time of year, which coincidentally takes place right at the end of the financial one. **Liz Blackman** (*Lab*) appeared to be a seasoned practitioner. In March 2005, she managed to get through all but the last £9 of that year's ACA allowance by snapping up a £199 DVD player and a £99 rug. In 2006, Ms. Blackman did even better: as April loomed, she filled her trolley with bed linen, towels, a new TV, a dishwasher and a (separate) fax machine, leaving just £2 of her allowance unspent.  By 2008 she was flagging slightly and returned home with nearly £500 of her ACA burning a hole in her handbag.

*"I'm sorry, sir, but I really cannot see how the purchase of a phoenix is essential to the performance of your duties – unless, of course, you're on the Opposition benches."*

# IN THEIR OWN WORDS

MPs are good at grovelling – that's how they get people to vote for them – but canvassing is nothing compared to the lengths they'll go to get round those pesky officials in the Fees Office. When caught red-handed on moot points of interpretation such as claiming for personal accountancy fees, or mixing up their mortgage payments, the most common excuse was to brush it off as "an unfortunate administrative error".

**Sir Gerald Kaufman** (*Lab*) A note on file at the Fees Office records details of a telephone conversation with Mr. Kaufman in which he attempted to justify a £28,834 claim for a new kitchen and work on the bathroom of his apartment near Regent's Park. "Old flat, facilities out of date, decrepit, health reasons, update, living in slum". For the avoidance of confusion, it was the flat that was alleged to be decrepit.

**Sir Gerald Kaufman** (*again*) The veteran Socialist crusader reached breaking point when his claim for £1,262 against a gas bill that was £1,055.60 in credit was queried by the Fees Office. The hysterical retort: "I received a letter from [an official saying they would] not pay as is credit. I paid £1,252 THIS year so want reimbursing!!!" For what?

Maybe a clue lies in Sir Gerald's reasoning for claiming for two matching grapefruit bowls, one for each home. He blamed "self-diagnosed Obsessive Compulsive Disorder" saying his day would be thrown into turmoil if his breakfast wasn't identical wherever he consumed it. He went on to emphasize: "I live very modestly".

**Kitty Ussher** (*Lab*) Clearly a woman of style, Usher claimed £20,000 for a property makeover which included the blotting out of several '70s-style ceilings : "Most of the ceilings have Artex coverings. Three-dimensional swirls. It could be a matter of taste, but this counts as 'dilapidations' in my book!" snarled Ms. Usher, before pleading "Can the ACA pay for the ceilings to be plastered over and repainted?"

**Shahid Malik** (*Lab*) The Junior Justice Minister was rather miffed when the Fees Office turned down his request for £2,100 to cover the cost of a 40-inch plasma TV. "From a natural justice perspective", he wrote to the bean counters in March 2006, "I feel a justifiable exception would be the fairest manner to deal with the current situation". A compromise was eventually reached whereby Mr. Malik received half the cost of the state-of-the-art machine.

## Pleading Poverty...
**Jeff Ennis** (*Lab*) "My bath has been condemned" he whimpered when claiming £85 for plumbing costs.

**Andy Burnham** (*Lab*) "I would be very grateful if [the expenses] could be paid in the last round of the year on Friday. Otherwise I might be in line for a divorce!" wrote Burnham after putting in a claim for £16,500 against his London flat in 2005. Mrs. B is clearly not to be messed with.

**Fabian Hamilton** (*Lab*) "I appreciate you are under severe pressure... but, as I explained on the phone, I am away for two weeks and I don't want to leave my family destitute".

**Anonymous Labour MP** "I object to your decision not to reimburse me for the costs of purchasing a baby's cot for use in my London home... Perhaps you might write to me explaining where my son should sleep next time he visits me in London?"

## ...and Bleeding Incompetence
**Jack Straw** (*Lab*) "... accountancy does not appear to be my strongest suit", Mr. Straw wrote after claiming the full amount of council tax on his Blackburn home despite having only had to pay 50% of the bill. A good thing he never made it to The Treasury then.

**Taxing Issues**

The incumbent Chancellor, **Alistair Darling,** and old Cabinet sparring partner Transport Secretary **Geoff Hoon** are obviously above such matters as who should pay for their personal 'tax advice' and other issues of interest to the Treasury, such as Stamp Duty, attributing their claims to "inadvertent administrative errors". Hoon it seems cannot even count beyond one, having claimed for three TV licences in a single year. Thank your lucky stars, then, he's no longer at the MOD.

**Just for the Record**

The self justifications haven't been restricted to communication with the Fees Office. When the *Telegraph* outed **Austin Mitchell** (*Lab*) for claiming £1,200 for the cost of having his sofas reupholstered, he wrote a letter to the newspaper explaining his action in the following terms:

"The sofas came with the flat twenty years ago. Since great holes had appeared in the covers, which were stained with Branston Pickle, whisky and gin (*see* **Snouts in the Trough**), I decided that they would be detrimental to my career plans which at that stage involved inviting Neil Kinnock, Roy Hattersley and Peter Mandelson round for drinks and bananas to impress them with my potential. We therefore had them reupholstered (the sofas, that is, not Kinnock and Hattersley) which is surely more sensible, environmentally friendly and a damn sight less expensive than buying new ones. You should consider me for a conservation award".

Other MPs adopted less cuddly tones when confronted by the Press. When challenged by a journalist about the purchase of a £250 alarm clock (*see* **Never Knowingly Underclaimed**), **Michael Connarty** (*Lab*) replied "We didn't set up this system", leaving everyone wondering who he thought did. "Are we only allowed to buy things from the 99p store?" he added bitterly.

# WHO SAID WHAT?

**After the Great Expenses Scandal story broke, there was an unseemly scrummage to get to be seen in a good light. Can you match the following quotes to their owners?**

A. "I am angry and appalled. If my parents thought that these things were going on in the House of Commons they would be appalled"

B. "Politicians have done things that are unethical and wrong. I don't care if they were within the rules – they were wrong".

C. "Do I think this was a train crash waiting to happen? Yes, clearly it was. What we are seeing now is the unravelling of a system that thrived in the shadows".

D. "I have made a ridiculous and grave error of judgment. I am ashamed and humiliated and I apologise. As has been reported my claim for for the duck house was rightly 'not allowed' by the Fees Office".

E. "I'm as straight as they come".

F. "I've had a good innings, there is no bitterness, but as the saying goes, all political careers end in tears".

G. "I can hardly believe the number of thieves, liars and tax fiddlers who are still in post".

H. "Like Tony Blair, I don't mind people getting filthy rich. But I do object to them getting rich filthily".

I. "The atmosphere in Westminster is unbearable. People are constantly checking to see if others are ok. Everyone fears a suicide. If someone isn't seen, offices are called and checked".

J. "The outpouring of fury we've witnessed has been like a spring revolution".

CHOICES ARE:

Shahid Mallik

Anthony Steen

Nadine Dorries

Ann Widdecombe

David Cameron

Gordon Brown

Peter Viggers

Nick Clegg

Alan Duncan

Lord Tebbit

*answers*   A. Gordon Brown; B. David Cameron; C. Nick Clegg; D. Peter Viggers; E. Shahid Mallik, F. Anthony Steen; G. Ann Widdecombe; H. Lord Tebbit; I. Nadine Dorries; J. Alan Duncan

# PAYBACK TIME!

When all the fun was over, it was payback time. Our MPs, chequebooks (or in some cases small change) in hand, formed orderly queues at the Fees Office to make amends. Of course, in no sense should this newfound largesse be regarded as any kind of admission of conscious wrongdoing.

Here's a sample of who's giving back what:

**Sir John Butterfill** (*Con*): £60,000 for failure to pay Capital Gains Tax on £600,000 profit from house sale.

**Phil Hope** (*Lab*): £41,709 claimed for furniture and fittings to second home.

**Jonathan Djanogly** (*Con*): £25,000 for 'excessive' cleaning and gardening costs.

**Margaret Moran** (*Lab*): £22,500 for dry rot treatment.

**Elliot Morley** (*Lab*): £16,800 for charges against a repaid mortgage.

**Hazel Blears** (*Lab*): £13,332 for unpaid Capital Gains Tax.

**Sir Alan Haselhurst** (*Con*): £12,000 for gardening costs.

**Greg Barker** (*Con*): £10,000 of tax for sale of two properties.

**Sir Peter Viggers** (*Con*): £10,000 for 'excessive' gardening expenses.

**Michael Gove** (*Con*): £7,567 costs of refurbishing second home.

**Mark Hendrick** (*Lab*): £6,850 for claiming costs against two homes.

**John Bercow** (*Con*): £6,500 for unpaid Capital Gains Tax.

**Ronnie Campbell** (*Lab*): £6,200 of furniture expenses for his second home.

**Hilary Armstrong** (*Lab*): £5,500 for grocery bills.

**Alan Duncan** (*Con*): £5,000 for gardening expenses.

**Richard Younger-Ross** (*Lib Dem*): £4,333 for luxury furniture purchases.

**Peter Luff** (*Con*): £3,185 for multiple second home expenses.

**Tony McNulty** (*Lab*): £3,055 for erroneous mortgage claims.

**Gareth Thomas** (*Lab*): £2,800 for duplicate mortgage claim and gardening costs.

**Lady Sylvia Hermon** (*UUP*): £2,730 overpayment of rental allowance.

**Mark Lazarowicz** (*Lab*): £2,675 fees for extending his second home.

**Andrew Lansley** (*Con*): £2,600 for decorating second home (Farrow & Ball no less) immediately before selling it.

**David Kidney** (*Lab*): £2,450 for council tax errors.

**Ed Vaizey** (*Lab*): £2,268 for antique furniture for his second home.

**Douglas Hogg** (*Con*): £2,200 for the cost of cleaning that moat.

**Oliver Letwin** (*Con*): £2,145 for fixing a leaking pipe under his tennis court.

**Linda Gilroy** (*Lab*): £1,891 for overclaimed council tax.

**Gerald Kaufman** (*Lab*): The frugal liver coughed up £1,851 for an antique rug imported from the US.

**Shahid Malik** (*Lab*): is donating £1,050 to charity.

**Julia Goldsworthy** (*Lib Dem*): £1,005 for purchase of a pink rocking chair.

**Diana Johnson** (*Lab*): £987 for architects' fees.

**Alistair Darling** (*Lab*): £668 for second home service charges over a three-month period.

**David Cameron** (*Con*): £680 for removal of vines.

**George Osborne** (*Con*): £440.62 for a single taxi journey.

**Jeff Hoon** (*Lab*): £384 for advance payment of household bills.

**Stewart Jackson** (Con): £304 for work on his swimming pool.

**Alistair Burt** (*Con*): £229 for snacks and drinks purchased while staying at hotels.

**Liam Byrne** (*Lab*): £240 for envelopes used to distribute publicity material.

**Fraser Kemp** (*Lab*): £212 for claims for two DVD players in one month.

**Gordon Brown** (*Lab*): £153 for double-charged plumbing costs.

**Alan Beith** (*Lib Dem*): £140 of second home allowances.

**Chris Huhne** (*Lib Dem*): £119 for a trouser press.

**Michael Ancram** (*Con*): £98.85 for swimming pool heater repairs.

**Nick Clegg** (*Lib Dem*): £80 for phone calls to friends and family.

**Andrew George** (*Lib Dem*): £20 for a hotel breakfast.

**Cheryl Gillan** (*Con*): £4.47 for dog food.

**Mike Penning** (*Con*): £2.99 for the purchase of a dog bowl.

And, finally:

**Austin Mitchell** (*Lab*), who, having claimed £1,200 for having his sofas reupholstered, has kindly offered to donate the old covers to the *Telegraph*.

### Who Knows?
Tony Blair's claim for £260 for shredding confidential data was unlikely to be paid back. While completely unconnected, Mr. Blair's receipts covering £43,029 of claims during a three-year period were sadly unavailable for scrutiny, as officials said they had been shredded in error.

"Well, I don't understand it. They all seemed quite keen
on the idea when I suggested it."

# WHY DOESN'T THIS HAPPEN ELSEWHERE?

Well, of course it does, but very rarely does the entire governing body of a nation get outed all at the same time. Maybe that's because the British like to do things in style. Or maybe it's because the British on the whole don't take politicians as seriously as the politicians themselves would like to think, and hence have let them get away with blue murder for years.

### Stateside

In the USA, freedom of information and the public scrutiny of almost all things paid for by the taxpayer is a well-established tradition. It wasn't always so. In 1992, the 'Rubbergate' scandal rocked the Washington boat in a manner not dissimilar to the recent Westminster debacle. The US House of Representatives operated the House Bank as a clearing facility for members' expenses, but unfortunately allowed many to become wildly overdrawn. When the scandal broke, 22 House members were named by the House Ethics committee, four were prosecuted, and a total of 77 either resigned or were run out of office in the 1994 election.

Still, when it comes to property, American Congressmen and Senators often really do need second homes in Washington as their constituencies can be thousands of miles away. Uncle Sam has, however, devised a neat solution to the expenses issue. Representatives are paid more than our beloved MPs ($174,000 as of 2009, which equates to around £116,000) but not given so much as a nickel for their living and housing expenses. The assumption is that they should pay for such things out of their salaries like everyone else.

Mind you, they do get mind-blowing office allowances. If the staffing arrangements of Euro MPs sound generous (*see* **Our**

**Colleagues Over There**), consider the bonanza on offer on Capitol Hill. Members of the US House of Representatives get office allowances ranging between US$ 1.3 million and US$ 1.9 million per year, depending on factors such as the distance between their constituencies and Washington. This would be considered small change to Senators, who receive staffing allowances of between US$2.9 and US$4.5 million.

### Further Afield

In Japan, MPs are paid more than twice as much as their impoverished British equivalents (around £215,000 when bonuses are taken into account) but this generosity doesn't extend to housing. Out-of-towners are provided with accommodation in Tokyo but it is far from glamorous - they are squeezed into student-style halls of residence.

The Swedes keep their politicians on a tight leash. Travel expenses are paid, for example, but MPs must use the cheapest possible methods of getting from A to B and book their tickets through the parliamentary travel office. The rules regarding accommodation are equally strict. Parliament owns around 250 flats in Stockholm, in which members from outside the capital are allowed to stay rent free, but if they choose to make their own arrangements they receive a measly £560 a month and aren't allowed to claim for home improvements. The electorate will tolerate no nonsense from its politicians. Sometimes it won't even apply common sense. When Deputy Prime Minister Mona Sahlin was caught buying nappies with her ministerial credit card in 1995, the ensuing furore forced her to resign from the Cabinet.

French Deputies have perks coming out of their ears. They get free first-class travel on the French rail network and unaudited allowances for transport, clothes and the throwing of receptions. They can also still go to the Assembly building after losing their seats, which allows them to indulge in the lucrative business of lobbying.

# OUR COLLEAGUES OVER THERE

Anyone who wants to feel better about British MPs just has to consider their equivalents in Brussels. Members of the European Parliament have tried to suppress details of their expenses claims – in March 2009 70% of them voted to keep them secret – but the truth will (sometimes) out. The extent to which MEPs are able and often inclined to milk the system was revealed in a top secret report written by EU Internal Audit Official Robert Gilpin in 2006. The document's findings might never have come to light – even MEPs were only allowed to read it in a locked and guarded room – had not Chris Davies MEP (*Lib Dem*) revealed its existence to the world in 2008. Fortunately, someone has since been responsible enough to leak the report to the press.

## Comedy of Errors

The Gilpin report is based on a sample of 167 of 4,686 payments made in October 2004. One shudders to think what he may have missed and how much worse things may have become since. The lowlights include the following:

- Payments were found to have been made to assistants not accredited to the European Parliament and to companies whose accounts showed a conspicuous lack of other activity.

- Payments designated as 'secretarial work' were made to a crèche whose manager turned out to be a politician from the political party of the MEP in question.

- Bonuses worth more than one and a half times annual salary were paid to assistants. Some rocket scientists have speculated that this was to enable members to use up their full annual allowance.

- Some relatives, sorry assistants, doubled their earnings by pocketing pay-offs from outgoing MEPs at the same time as salaries from new ones.

– One MEP claimed to have paid the full staff allowance (then £182,000) to one individual. The report thought it not implausible that this was a relative.

– Direct payments were made into the bank accounts of national political parties.

### Eat Your Way to a Million

The Taxpayers' Alliance has since painted a vivid picture of how an MEP on the fiddle could pocket over £1.1 million in the course of a five-year term of office (that's pocket, not just claim). The breakdown, which assumed that the Euro representative in question was actually making some legitimate use of his or her allowances in addition to salting some away, included dipping into the following:

- £259 daily subsistence allowance (not bad if you stay with a friend and eat at bog standard bistros). You just have to turn up and sign in to demonstrate that you have 'attended'.

- Up to £90,000 annual travel allowance (members are assumed to purchase open economy tickets and get an additional sum based on distance travelled. No receipts required).

- £217,800 over five years if main home was also designated as a constituency office (no receipts required).

- Nearly £230,000 staff/office expenses (until recently family members could be employed with impunity). UK MEPs were found to be the worst offenders.

- When an MEP leaves office a 'transition' payment of £41,573 is built into their package.

- They could also look forward to a pension pot worth approximately 350K at the end of a 5-year term.

### Other freebies include:

- Up to 60 mud baths, or hydro-massages, or hydrotherapy or acupuncture sessions per annum, if recommended by a doctor's note.

- Dental surgery worth £150 per gold crown.

- Contact lenses, batteries for hearing aids and bandages for varicose veins (presumably an occupational hazard from carrying all that loot).

- Language and IT courses are thrown in up to a cost of £5,885.

No receipts need to be submitted, just claims within the allowable expense bands.

British MEPs still feeling hard done-by could comfort themselves with the thought of a net pay rise of almost 50 per cent due to kick in after the June 2009 European Elections, hoisting them to a comfortable annual salary of £83,282 (with income tax at a crippling 15%).

## Bend Over, Dover

One of them, however, has been busted with his hands in the till – surprising when you consider what is available quite legitimately. In November 2008, **Den Dover** (*Con*) was ordered to pay back around £500,000 of some £750,000 of Euro-allowances that he was alleged to have paid into a family firm called M.P. Holdings Ltd. over the course of nine years.

## What a Waste?

MEP **Dr. Caroline Jackson** (*Con*), one of Euro-Parliament's advisors on waste management, simply wasn't up to the job when it came to producing an exhaustive 15-page booklet on the subject. So she called in some expert help in the form of her husband, former MP Robert. After much tricky negotiation, "an appropriate professional fee" was agreed, a mere £22,500. As the booklet includes the cover (with a nice photo of a landfill on the front), a blank page, an introduction running to two full sentences, and a final page of Dr. Jackson's contact details, it works out that she paid him £2,250 per page. One wonders if anybody found the time to read it – it probably went straight into the recycling bin.

## Do They Mean Us?

The consensus of opinion beyond these shores is that the British have gone mad (again). One Dutchman wrote to *The Times* saying "Here in the Netherlands we laugh at this typical hysterical witch-hunt... Your TV channels show the mob in the street demanding to build a gallows in the market square. Pathetic and primitive. Once again Britain is the laughing stock of Europe".

*"I love these little trips. Remind me, what facts are we finding today?"*

### In Continents

MPs like to travel. One of the most frequently cited examples of the abuse of the public's hard-earned cash has been the 'junket', or to use it's more formal name, the 'Fact-Finding Mission'. Sometimes linked to major international conferences (with all the trimmings: banquets, five-star hotels, after dinner politicking in the bar etc.) where Westminster feels it's presence needs to be felt, these more commonly take the form of a sort of free holiday (again in commensurate accommodation, preferably near a beach or pool) which involves little more than some inconvenient photoshoots with the unfortunate flyblown inhabitants of an underdeveloped country.

# FALLOUT

It would be misleading to say that the dust settled rapidly in the aftermath of the Great British Expenses Scandal – the newspapers kept all kinds of revelations up their sleeves for rainy days – but some of the consequences immediately became clear. They fell under three main headings: rumbled MPs falling on their swords, foreigners having a good laugh at our expense and the electorate becoming worryingly disenchanted with mainstream politicians.

### Who's Stepping Down
Prominent casualties of the scandal included:

**Michael Martin** (*Lab*) When the extent of his failure to prevent abuses of the expenses system became clear (let alone his inability to prevent the scandal hitting the headlines in the first place), Mr. Martin became the first Speaker of the Commons to be forced out of office since John Trevor in 1695.

**Shalid Malik** (*Lab*) became the first minister to step down after it emerged that he had nominated a £100-a-week flat in his Dewsbury constituency as his main residence while claiming £66,827 over three years for a 'second home' in London. He was later reinstated.

**Jacqui Smith** (*Lab*) After revelations that she had designated her sister's house as her main home and got the taxpayer to pay for her husband's porn videos, it was only a matter of time before Ms. Smith realized she had little option but to step down as Home Secretary.

**Hazel Blears** (*Lab*) The feisty serial-flipping 'chipmunk' resigned as Communities Secretary "to return to the grassroots where I began". She didn't exit gracefully, lambasting her leader in public, and flouting a brooch with the motto 'Rocking the Boat' – although strangely retracting her comments a matter of days later.

**Elliot Morley** (*Lab*) Having been busted for claiming £16,000 for a non-existent mortgage, the former Environment Minister announced his intention to step down at the next election.

**Julie Kirkbride** (*Con*) After getting the taxpayer to pay (among other things) £50,000 for an extension to her constituency flat and £540 for publicity photographs of her disporting herself amongst bales of hay, the Bromsgrove MP bowed to the inevitable.

**Andrew MacKay** (*Con*) The Tory heavyweight resigned as an aide to party leader David Cameron after it emerged that he and his wife Julie Kirkbride (*see above*) had made claims on both their homes.

**Ben Chapman** (*Lab*) sensibly decided to avoid the embarrassment of standing at the next election after being caught claiming £15,000 interest charges on a paid-off mortgage.

**Sir Peter Viggers** (*Con*) Having secured immortality through his duck house claim, Viggers proclaimed that he would quit at the next election.

**Douglas Hogg** (*Con*) As a result of 'Moatgate', Hogg decided he would raise the drawbridge and lower the portcullis at the next election.

**Nicholas** (71) and **Ann Winterton** (68, both *Con*) Two more of the Tory old guard whose names will not be appearing on future ballot papers, the Wintertons were found to have claimed £80,000 for the rental of a London flat owned by a trust controlled by their offspring. For years they had flaunted a high on the hog lifestyle – to such an extent that they were nicknamed 'Mr. & Mrs. Expenses'. The couple had consistently voted against reforming the expenses system. In order to avoid losing face, their joint statement stressed their years of service, but "maybe the years are taking their toll... we have reached the conclusion that we should pass on the baton to a younger person because both Congleton and Macclesfield deserve the very best".

# DISCLOSURE

**The Great Expenses Scandal was unfortunately not really a 'disaster waiting to happen'. The levels of duplicity certain MPs were prepared to sink to had already become clear many years earlier when MPs had been forced to declare any other sources of income (in cash or kind) that they received. This act of disclosure produced a number of loud "Harrumphs" in Westminster clubland, and not a few red faces along the way.**

In 2007-2008, **David Cameron** was the lucky recipient of a sterling silver tray from George W. Bush, a rug from the former Prime Minister of Pakistan, a Harrods hamper from the Sultan of Brunei and a fountain pen, cufflinks and studs from the King of Bahrain. And he's not alone: a good many of our MPs have goods and services thrust upon them from their adoring public – or wads of cash from those who just want to make sure that their party has enough money to fund those extravagant election campaigns. To steer clear of any allegations of bribery or worse, MPs must be scrupulously transparent in declaring such gifts and are bound by strict rules. At the beginning of 2008, 24 MPs received stiff letters from the Electoral Commission for failing to declare gifts, donations and free trips abroad to a combined value of £251,000 within the four-week time limit. Among those admonished were **Michael Howard** (*Con*), **Nick Clegg** (*Lib Dem*), **Boris Johnson** (*Con*), **Alan Milburn** (*Lab*) and the 'gifted' **David Willetts** (*Con*).

**Here are a few others who have felt their collars pinched:**
In April 2004, **Jack Straw** (*Lab*) decided to celebrate the silver anniversary of his entry into Parliament with a little bash at Blackburn Rovers' Ewood Park stadium where, for a mere £25 a head, guests were treated to a thrilling pictorial romp through the MP's career. Any warm glow Mr. Straw felt after the event was abruptly put out three years later when the little matter of the evening's sponsorship came to light. Canatxx Energy Ventures confirmed that it had put £3,000 towards the event but

somehow the money had neither gone through the local party's bank account nor been declared under Party rules. The Justice Secretary was ultimately let off after a grovelling apology and a dressing-down from the Standards and Privileges Committee.

In 2007, **Peter Hain** (*Lab*) set his sights on the Deputy Leadership of the Labour Party and set about raising a bit of cash to fund his campaign. An impressive £103,000 worth of donations rolled in. Rather less impressive was his failure to declare the cash within the time limit required under the Political Parties Elections and Referendums Act (introduced by his own party in 2000). When Scotland Yard were called in to investigate, Mr. Hain resigned as Work and Pensions Secretary and slunk off into the political shadows. A lengthy Crown Prosecution Service enquiry, at a cost of some £250,000 to the taxpayer, found insufficient evidence to charge the forgetful MP with deliberate wrongdoing and he found himself reinstated to the Cabinet in Gordon Brown's June 2009 reshuffle as Welsh Secretary.

**Lord Peter Mandelson** (*Lab*), forced out of office in 1998 for failing to declare a £373,000 loan from a Parliamentary colleague, should be first in the queue when it comes to reporting items of personal benefit. Ten years later, the then Mr. Mandelson found himself in hot water again over an evening of entertainment aboard the superyacht of Russian oligarch, Oleg Deripaska. Not only were eyebrows raised about the value of the hospitality Mandelson had enjoyed, there was also the awkward question of what the UK's European Trade Commissioner was doing hobnobbing with the 'king of aluminium' when his own department was making decisions that benefited that particular line of business. The European Parliament has since commissioned a report looking into such ethical conundrums, which it hopes to publish sometime in 2009.

Many British National Party supporters crave anonymity – wouldn't you? – particularly where party donations are concerned. In 2009, the party's leader **Nick Griffin** found himself facing a challenge when a little old lady presented him with a cheque for £5,000, but did not want her allegiance made public. Electoral Commission rules state that any donation of over £1,000 made to an individual party member must be declared. Mr Griffin rested the money in his personal account for a while before coming up with the idea of transferring it to a trade union with strong BNP links, thereby sidestepping the authorities. The Electoral Commission is looking into the matter.

So, the Wheel of Fortune (or is that Fate?) turns. The British public might understandably ask, "What next?" And equally understandably expect to see an answer.

*"I really don't see why we have to wear these armbands just because we made an unfortunate administrative error".*

# AND FINALLY...

It has been said that the only person to enter the Houses of Parliament with honourable intentions was Guido Fawkes — and look what happened to him. Let's hope better fates await the following (all on current salaries of £64,766).

**Adam Afriyie** (*Con, elected 2005*)
Total second home claims to date: £0.00.

**Tom Brake** (*Lib Dem*)
Total second home claims since 2004/2005: £0.00.

**Susan Kramer** (*Lib Dem*)
Total second home claims since 2006/2006: £0.00
(2004/2005 unavailable).

**Ed Davey** (*Lib Dem*)
Total second home claims since 2004/2005: £0.00.

Millionaire and generous friend of Peter Mandelson
**Geoffrey Robinson** (*Lab*)
Total second home claims since 2004/2005: £0.00.

**Congratulations!**

**Plus One Also-ran:**
**James Brokenshire** (*Con, Shadow Home Affairs Minister*)
Total second home claims since 2004/2005: £368.00.

**Consolation Prize for the Smallest Members' Claim**
The Shadow Culture Secretary **Jeremy Hunt** managed to claw back 1p for a 12-second mobile phone call.

# COMING CLEAN?

"Transparency to the public is the foundation of properly policing this system", Gordon Brown.

Laundry

57-50

lost receipt

Mr G. Brown

Monday 14th May

Invoice no
Week ending Friday 18th May 2007

=£63.
=£73.50

£534-75

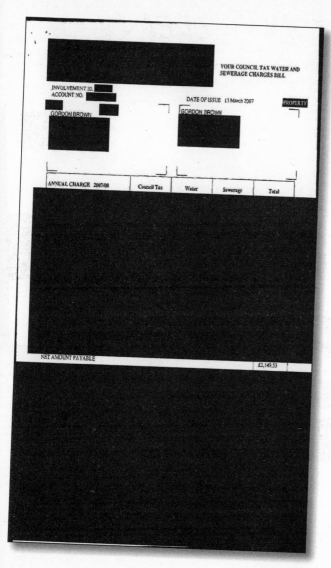

YOUR COUNCIL TAX WATER AND
SEWERAGE CHARGES BILL

INVOLVEMENT ID.
ACCOUNT NO.

DATE OF ISSUE   13 March 2007

PROPERTY

GORDON BROWN

GORDON BROWN

| ANNUAL CHARGE   2007/08 | Council Tax | Water | Sewerage | Total |
|---|---|---|---|---|

NET AMOUNT PAYABLE                                              £2,149.53

· P. brueghel · Inuentor ·                    Cock · exeud · cum priuileg · 1558 ·

# PART TWO:
# GREED: A BRIEF HISTORY

Of course, venality in public office is nothing new. It has a
long and venerable history – it may indeed lay claim to really
being the 'World's Oldest Profession'. Way back in the 16th
century, Pieter Bruegel the Elder described exquisite punish-
ments for the money-hungry who populated his society
(*above*). Sadly, such recourses are rarely available to us today.
In this section we provide an abbreviated survey of the wide
range of ways pockets can be lined at others' expense.

# EMPIRES OF EXCESS

The precedents for our hapless MPs stretch far back into the past, and many of their forebears make our current miscreants look like rank amateurs. It goes without saying that being (or proclaiming yourself) an emperor immediately outranks a mere MP, and helps enormously when it comes to dealing with the likes of the Fees Office. Here are a few who really knew how to shoulder the burden of spending the public's money creatively.

## Taking it into the Afterlife

While many of our current MPs are probably thinking in a more short-term manner, at best worrying over the pensions and at least over their weekly Waitrose bills, the originators of the 'big spend' tended to invest pretty heavily in what would happen after they dropped off the mortal coil. Most notorious among these were the Egyptian pharaohs who, not content with living a life of considerable luxury whilst still on the mortal coil, invested huge amounts of dosh on impenetrable pyramid tombs, which they promptly filled with huge quantities of furniture, food and utensils to accompany them into the next world. And, of course, gold; in fact, so keen were they on the stuff that they bypassed the public taxation system altogether and simply conquered the desert wastes of Nubia (where the best local gold mines were) to ensure an almost limitless supply.

The Egyptians didn't, however, loot on quite the same scale as the Persians, whose bully-boy tactics enabled them to conquer most of Central Asia, and then demand 'tribute' from the various representatives of their dominions. So exacting were they in their demands that the now ruined imperial capital of Persepolis was lined with relief carvings reminding their various governors of what they were expected to cough up every year.

## The Glory That Was Rome

Originating as a bunch of freebooters in the western Mediterranean 2,500 years ago, Rome and its rulers soon developed aspirations to greatness. Interestingly, **Octavian** (27 BC-AD 14), the first self-proclaimed emperor, renaming himself Emperor Augustus, apparently lived a frugal life. It didn't cost him or the Romans much for Augustus to proclaim that the god Apollo was on his payroll, and he lavishly spent public funds on public projects, building the Ara Pacis and the Forum of Augustus and patronizing Virgil and other masters of the art of sucking up to the one who was on the throne.

Augustus established a kind of benchmark for how to behave in public office, even if you were a Supreme Being. He assumed that monuments like memorial arches and triumphal columns would be erected by a grateful populace some time after he had crossed the River Styx. In fact the senate went one better, and proclaimed him a god after his demise. It was Augustus's successors who really took advantage of their position: his grandnephew **Nero** (AD 54-68), threw up a massive 'Golden House' on the edge of the Forum, while a few years later **Hadrian** (AD 117-138) not only built a wall in a completely useless place but taxed the Roman exchequer to build himself a sort of Playboy Mansion in Tivoli, almost a square mile of buildings, pools and gardens well beyond the urban stinkpot of Rome, where he could disport himself at water-games, pretend sea battles and, presumably, full-on orgies – all on his imperial expense account.

### The Middle Ages

This kind of behaviour set something of a pattern amongst other aspiring world rulers. Ignoring the ignominious fall of Rome in the 5th century, the rulers of the predominant Islamic states which emerged in the early 8th century were pretty keen on the good life, building new cities and throwing up palaces and luxuriant gardens across Eurasia, always in the shadow, naturally, of some magnificent mosques to keep everybody happy.

The Mongol ruler of China, Genghis Khan's grandson Kublai Khan, built up a court at his new capital of Khanbalik that was the envy of simply everyone, the splendour of the place becoming so legendary that it encouraged Venetian merchant Marco Polo and his dad to travel all the way across Asia on not just one, but two extended visits, keen to negotiate trade concessions. Five hundred years later, Kublai Khan's HQ was still being cited by the likes of Coleridge as the example of profligate luxury.

## How to Build Your Own Empire

When **Christopher Columbus** stumbled across the Americas *en route* to Asia he stumbled on a pot of gold (almost literally), and inaugurated an unseemly scramble among the then peripheral nations of Europe to conquer and squeeze the pips out of the rest of the world. His patrons, the Spanish, lost no time in beating the local Indians into submission and filling hundreds of galleons with (the natives') gold and silver. The French weren't quite as keen then on overseas empires as their neighbours, as **Louis XIV** managed to extract enough funds from his own subjects to build the world's largest palace at Versailles.

But other Europeans soon jumped on the colonial bandwagon, not least the British.

The development of the British Empire was largely dependent on:

- Establishing a tentative trading foothold overseas (a technique learned from the Portuguese).

- Intimidating (or slaughtering) the local population (a technique learned from the Spanish).

- Assuming control of international trade in the most profitable local products (learned from the Dutch).

- Letting a 'chap I knew at school' take control (learned from nobody else, just based on a uniquely British clubbish 'Gentlemen's Agreement').

Thus were brought into being several generations of rapine freebooters who soon evolved into celebrated heroes of the Empire. **Walter Raleigh** set the trend in Virginia in the 16th century – for which he lost his head – but the roll of honour later included such stalwarts as **Clive of India**, **Raffles** (founder of Singapore), 'Rajah' **James Brooke** of Sarawak and **Cecil Rhodes** in southern Africa.

Whilst not exactly ripping the British public off, these guys were experts at using Britain's wealth, military and naval muscle and resources to carve out private empires overseas whilst piling up the cash they acquired. It is futile to try to assess exactly what they extracted for their coffers, but it ran into hundreds of millions at today's prices. Rhodes was reckoned to be one of the richest men in the world by the time of his death in 1902. **King Leopold of Belgium** outstripped them all by annexing the whole of the Congo for his newly-independent country, and set about turning it into a private fiefdom designed to generate as much cash as possible at whatever cost to the local inhabitants.

### Rule Britannia

While the slave trade allowed many to build substantial fortunes out of plantations in far-flung places supplying British industrialists with sugar, cotton and tobacco, (and as if the legacy of tobacco wasn't enough) the British also came up with another interesting wheeze. Having led the campaign to ban slavery, they then hatched a plan to turn the world's largest country – China – into a nation of opium addicts, while controlling their supplies. It led to a couple of wars, but – hey – it made millions for the pedlars involved.

So, are our politicians that bad, do they set their sights too low, or have they simply had bad teachers?

# KLEPTOCRATS

The tune to which the British public were ripped off by their elected representatives pales into very trivial insignificance when compared with the sheer scale and audacity of some of their peers overseas. Siphoning a nation's wealth into private tax-exempt offshore accounts became an essential skill on many a wannabe international statesman's CV – and not just in the 'Developing World'. But it does seem that enjoying the support of 'the West' is often a useful endorsement for pillaging a nation's cashflow.

Here are just a few of the worst offenders:

**Estimated US$15-35 billion**
**Mohamed Suharto (1921-2008), President of Indonesia, 1967-98**
Admittedly, Mr. Suharto was in a position to milk his country of funds for longer than many of his rivals, but the scale of his asset-stripping was impressive, to say the least. An electorally unopposed autocrat, supported by the West after his vicious suppression of Communist elements in his sprawling country in the 1960s, it was only after his resignation in 1998 at the age of 77 that the hoard accumulated by his family began to be investigated.

In 1999, *Time Asia* estimated the Suharto's wealth at US$15 billion in cash (with US$9 billion already being deposited in European banks), plus thousand of acres of land-holdings and office real estate, including some 40% of the disputed island of East Timor – no wonder he resisted their independence movement. Minor mysteries such as the disappearance of some US$300 million from a scholarship fund, and the embezzlement of over US$530 million of government funds allegedly channelled into various family-controlled charities, seemed like just drops in the ocean.

By the time the Indonesian judiciary had accumulated enough evidence to mount a prosecution, Suharto was declared too ill to be tried. It was later revealed that the family sweetened the legal system with US$600,000-worth of bribes, but Suharto died unprosecuted in 2008, although his son Hutomo ('Tommy') and half-brother Probosutedjo were both jailed on charges including land scams, misappropriation of charitable funds and, in Tommy's case, arranging the murder of a judge.

## US$5-10 billion
### Ferdinand Marcos (1917-89), President of The Philippines, 1965-86

America's puppet ruler of their main Southeast Asian power base in the latter years of the Vietnam War was ironically far less notorious for his greed than his shoe-collecting wife, Imelda. His strong-man personality cult (he had been prosecuted for murder as a young man) and ruthless suppression of political rivals provided a protective screen. But, as US support for his regime waned, and demands for democratic elections increased, Marcos and his wife fled to a safe haven in the offshore US state of Hawaii (a resort guaranteed by the then president, US Ronald Reagan). In doing so, some interesting spoils were revealed: sadly Imelda had to abandon 2,500 pairs of shoes back in Manila (they just wouldn't fit in her suitcase), while US Customs officials in Honolulu recorded 24 suitcases of gold blocks and jewellery (hidden in nappy bags) and gold bullion certificates running into yet more billions of dollars. Even today, the Philippine government continues to pay interest on the US$28 billion national debt that Marcos ran up, and appears to have run off with.

## US$5 billion
### Mobutu Sese Seko (1930-97), President of Zaire, 1965-97

Seizing power in a CIA-sponsored coup, Mobutu set himself up as a bastion against Communism in the dark heart of Africa, and continued to foster close relations with the USA, Belgium, France and the International Monetary Fund, despite an appalling human rights record, whilst simultaneously boosting a fervent African (and racist) nationalism. This disguised in large part his main activity – pouring money gained from nationalizing foreign-owned businesses, from international loans, and from liquidizing his country's considerable mineral assets into an array of Swiss bank accounts. While food was scarce, and public servants – even, eventually, the army – went largely unpaid (all, that is, except for his security service), Mobutu frequently hired an Air France Concorde for days, if not weeks, at a time to ferry him to foreign meetings and health clinics. The civil war from 1994 eventually forced the ailing Mobutu into exile to a health centre in Morocco 1997, where he fortunately had little time left to enjoy his ill-gotten gains.

## US$2-5 billion
### Sani Abacha (1943-98), President of Nigeria, 1993-98

'Scarface' was a soubriquet associated with US bootlegger, protectioneer, tax-evader and organized crime supremo Al Capone. Abacha probably didn't evade (or even need to pay) taxes, but his exploitation of his position as boss of the pivotal country in West Africa exceeded even Capone's capacity for money-gathering. And he had more facial scars to boot. Seizing power just as Nigeria's oil-boom was on the wane, Sani Abacha and his kin managed to skim a sizeable load of Nigeria's cash into offshore bank accounts. Although his son Mohammed maintains that these funds were "legitimately acquired" his family did agree in 2002 to pay back US$1.2 billion lifted from the Central Bank. Why? Unless, of course, the revenues from the all-too-familiar internet 'advance fee fraud' scams which frequently cite members of the Abacha family have not proved as lucrative as they might have hoped.

## US$1 billion
### Slobodan Milosevic (1941-2006), President of Serbia (1989-97)/'Yugoslavia' 1997-2000

A racist hoodlum, surrounded by an unsavoury bunch of thugs (prominently including a psychopathic military hero and a 'doctor') who attempted to weld together a multi-national state in Europe through 'ethnic cleansing' and outright villainy. Sounds familiar? Well, at least Mr. Hitler didn't seem to have been quite as interested in money as this cove. In a brief five years in the 1990s, Milosevic managed to spirit away around seven per cent

*"Look, matey, who's in charge here? I don't give a fig for what the manager says, send the bill direct to the Fees Office at the Senate".*

of Serbia's Gross National Product. Unfortunately, Mr. Milosevic died before he could conduct a reasonable defence of his actions before the International War Crimes Tribunal in The Hague.

## Other Contenders

Few (except perhaps the 50 million or so Iranians who supported the Islamic revolution which ousted him in 1979) would doubt that the late inhabitant of the 'Peacock Throne' of Persia, **Shah Mohammad Reza Pahlavi** was a considerable benefactor to his country. He introduced reforms in education, health, women's suffrage and, significantly, made Iran a major player in Middle Eastern geo-politics by rationalizing its oil industry. However, there is also little doubt that he usurped his father, collaborated with the West to oust the awkwardly populist Premier Mossadeq, and suppressed any opposition while living the high life. In 1971, to celebrate the 2,500th anniversary of the Persian monarchy, the Shah put on a spectacle bound to upset his many under-privileged subjects: a 160-acre enclave was constructed near the ancient ruined capital of Persepolis, involving three huge royal tents and 59 others organized in a mystical star-shape, decorated by Maison Jansen; chefs were flown in from Maxim's of Paris, and diners fed on peacock breasts off specially-commissioned Limoges plateware, whilst supping champagne from Baccarat crystal glasses. The whole shebang reportedly cost the country in excess of US$100 million; the Shah instructed his staff not to reveal the costs.

Upon the Shah's fall, next door (so to speak) in dictators' row, an unlikely peasant and youthful assassin by the name of **Saddam Hussein** was beginning to be seen by the West as a bulwark against Islamic fundamentalism. Leading Iraq into an heroic war against the revolutionary Iranians, which cost almost as many lives as Europe's First World War, Saddam cloaked his personal pogroms against dissenting Shi'a, Kurds and other tiresome tribal groups who wouldn't toe his line. For his crusading valour, Hussein was showered with gifts in the form of trade concessions, technical assistance, arms and all manner of sugared delights. No wonder then that this Arab redneck would eventually get above his station. His eventual slapping down by 'coalition forces' took 15 bloody years and many lives (including those of Saddam and many of his family), but not before the family had looted an estimated US$300 million from the West-funded war chest. Found cowering in a tunnel after his overthrow, Saddam had an emergency escape fund of US$750,000 in cash in his pocket. Nice money if you can get it.

The continuing wearisome presence of **Dr. Robert Mugabe** (b. 1924) as CEO of the once shining African nation of Zimbabwe would be a joke if it wasn't so appalling for his subjects. Having taken the 'Africans First' ticket as a way to winning at the polls, the good doctor then proceeded to deliver on his promises by violently evicting white farmers from their lands, causing a famine and his nation's ostracism from international trade. While Zimbabweans starved, and the economy went into superinflation, the doctor, his second wife Grace and his hefty entourage of security personnel were often to be seen shopping on the boulevards of Paris. With a loaf of bread costing a mere few thousand Zimbabwean dollars by 2002, and funds running perilously low for a jet-set pariah, the

scholarly Mugabe hit on another winning ticket: Print More
Money! At the time of writing, though thoroughly vilified by
the international community at large, little direct action has been
taken to curb the deluded geriatric's excesses. But don't worry, in
addition to the sumptuous palace he has constructed in his home
nation, he recently bought a little retirement hideaway in Hong
Kong for a snip at HK$45.24 million (US$5.8 million).

## Case Study: Brazil Nuts
## Estimated total: US$1 billion

**Fernando Collor de Mello** was Brazil's president from March
1990 until December 1992. During his election campaign, he
promoted himself as the *Caçador de Marajás* (the hunter of
maharajahs), painting himself as one who would fight against
the big corruption schemers in the country. However, Collor's
economic package, Plano Collor 1, was the beginning of one
of the country's biggest corruption scandals, and forced Brazil
into its longest recession in history.

Among the measures he introduced was the confiscation of
the public's saving accounts, arguing that this was necessary
to stabilize the nation's monthly 84% inflation rate. By the end
of March 1990, the Treasury Minister, Zélia Cardoso de Mello
(no relation, but who drafted the scheme), announced that 80%
of the money in Brazil would be frozen, today the equivalent
of about US$100 billion – 30% of the country's GDP. Although
understandably anxious, most of the public were convinced
that this was necessary for future prosperity, although days
before the implementation of the package prices of many
food products shot up 300%.

In May 1991, Collor's brother, Pedro, leaked a number of
documents to *Veja* (Brazil's most popular magazine) that
identified the President's campaign treasurer, Paulo
César Farias, as the owner of numerous dummy companies
abroad. Around US$1 billion in his offshore bank accounts
came from 'frozen' public money, a further US$8 million
from Brazilian businessmen. Allegedly, in the scheme

70% of the money went to Collor and 30% to Farias.

In September 1992, the Brazilian Congress voted on the possibility of impeachment – 441 members voting in favor and 38 against. Collor went on national television asking the population for support. In December, however, he resigned before the Senate voted for his impeachment, in order to try to preserve his political rights. Despite this, the Senate suspended them for eight years, but the Supreme Federal Tribunal went on to acquit him of the corruption charges. In spite of the scandal, Collor was elected senator in the northeastern state of Alagoas in 2006(most of which his family owns), and in 2009 he became the president of the Infrastructure Commission in the Senate.

Meanwhile, Farias fled to England and then Thailand, where Interpol found him and extradited him back to Brazil. In 1994, he was convicted to seven years in prison but was released the next year. Less than two years later, Farias and his girlfriend, Suzana Marcolino, were found dead. The investigation concluded that it was a crime of passion, in which she killed him and then herself. However, some years later it was found out that the judge in charge of the case received R$4 million (US$2 million) to arrive at the verdict.

Maybe Britain isn't so bad after all.

# NATIONAL SCANDALS

It's not just individuals that get caught out playing the game by different rules, it can be whole countries or, as often as not, publicly-funded institutions within those countries. But when in Rome...

## Don't Go There

Transparency International has done some good work bringing to our attention places where it might not be a bright idea to live, let alone to travel or do business. They use various criteria to assess the 'honesty' or corruption levels of a sample of 30 countries (out of a current total of 194) to produce a report, the *Corruption Perceptions Index* or *CPI*, which sets out to assess the "degree to which corruption is perceived to exist among public officials and politicians". A recent edition of the report nominated as the cleanest countries Denmark, Finland and New Zealand; at the dirty end of the list loitered the usual suspects, unsurprisingly: Iraq, Burma (Myanmar) and the popular pirate haven of Somalia. But remember – they only sampled 30 countries.

The same organization also publishes the popular *Bribe Payer's Index*. Most of us are used to getting the basic amenities even if we are down on our uppers but, where genuine poverty is a national issue, paying bribes to suppliers and public officials can be a daily matter of course. In 2007, it was found that up to half the households in Cameroon, Paraguay, Cambodia and Mexico had found themselves paying a bribe to officials in the previous year.

## Where Not to do Business

As few organizations would admit to paying or receiving off-the-record funds to secure contracts, Transparency International's *Global Corruption Report* was based on asking some 50 international companies if they felt they had lost business as a result of competitors paying bribes – and where. It seems that trying to do a commercial deal in Hong Kong could involve three times as much palm-greasing as in the UK. Some of the other results may, or may not, surprise you.

| Hong Kong | 66% |
| Brazil | 42% |
| France | 32% |
| Germany | 28% |
| Netherlands | 26% |
| UK | 22% |
| USA | 20% |

That said, of course needs must when dealing in places with a different moral, cultural and economic set of values to your own. When asked if companies were likely to consider paying bribes to secure overseas contracts, the Swiss, Swedes and Canadians emerged as the least likely (oddly closely followed by the UK), while in ascending order the Indians, Chinese, Russians and Italians admitted to being the most likely.

### On the Graft: A Quiz

It seems that the police are just as bad as the rest of us — in fact sometimes much worse (as if we hadn't known it all along). A survey of people who found themselves paying a bribe as a result of having their collar felt revealed some astonishing statistics. Can you match the percentages to the region?

North America — 20%
Western Europe — 32%
CIS (former Soviet Union) — 1%
Southeast Europe — 19%
Latin America — 2%
Africa — 16%
Asia-Pacific — 55%

*answers* North America 2%; Western Europe 1%; CIS (former Soviet Union) 20%; Southeast Europe 16%; Latin America 32%; Africa 55%; Asia-Pacific 19%

### The Whiff of Scandal

The best thing about public scandals is the fascinating way that they emerge out of left field, gain momentum by dark hints, rumour and whispered conversations, are immediately denied when the whispers get too loud, and then break — and everyone says "There you go, we knew that all along". Sometimes people come clean, sometimes there is an effective cover-up, but it's a fundamental law of nature that shit sticks.

### Cash-for-Honours

In 2006, Labour Prime Minister Tony Blair achieved the accolade of being the first UK premier to be interviewed by the police. The reason? The names of an inordinate number of individuals who had loaned funds or provided other services to the Labour Party kept cropping up on the PM's peerage lists. Fortunately for Tony, no evidence was found that any honours had been offered in return for their support, but it left a funny smell in Downing Street.

*"Look, I don't care what 'him upstairs' says— I paid for a bloody baronetcy, and I won't settle for less."*

### The Bofors Arms Deal

The squeaky-clean Swedes found themselves up to their necks
in it in the 1980s when it emerged that one of their national
treasures, trail-blazing arms firm Bofors, was enmired in an
international cash-for-deal scandal. The country in question
was India, who were seeking to acquire 155 field howitzers;
the government in question was that of Rajiv Gandhi, the
leader of the Indian National Congress Party; the size of the
contract on the table was US$155 million; the middle-man
was alleged to be an Italian. The stage was set for a romantic
opera of tragic proportions. The talk was of kickbacks to senior
Indian ministers (including the premier) but in 1991 a *deus
ex machina* occurred with Gandhi's assassination. The Indian
judiciary found little hard evidence to link him or his ministers
to corruption charges, although that Italian fled to Argentina,
which, of course, has no extradition arrangements with India.

### Oil-for-Food

In 1995, the United Nations brokered a deal during the
dramatic stand-off between the US and Saddam Hussein's
trade-embargoed regime in Iraq. It involved the controlled
exchange of Iraq's crude oil for basic foodstuffs for Saddam's
subjects. Simple enough, you might think, until a swarm of
officials got in on the act. As one might have expected when
dealing with Iraq back then, what seemed straightforward soon
became very messy: oil coupons were exchanged as bribes,
concessions were offered on oil contracts and kickbacks flowed
to food suppliers. It being a UN deal, the ramifications spread
far and wide, and damaged several in high office: the Indian
Foreign Minister Natwar Singh resigned, and even the then
Secretary-General of the UN, Kofi Annan, was implicated.

# CORPORATE HIGHWAYMEN

Immensely successful business moguls tend to set themselves up as easy targets for investigation. Many are of course completely clean, but a surprising number have fallen foul of temptation over the years – often assuming not only that early successes will buy cashflow *ad infinitum* (and continue to deserve reward) but, when the winds of fortune change, that they will be able to make good whatever funds they need to continue the lifestyles to which they have become accustomed. How the mighty are fallen... often dragging many down with them.

### The Fat of the Land

While the granddaddy of them all, oil tycoon, film-maker, airplane inventor, airline operator and *brassière* designer **Howard Hughes**, simply went mad and became a recluse (his fortune more or less intact), British tycoon **Robert Maxwell** seems to have gone mad but happily carried on operating in public life. After an heroic Second World War, Czech-born Maxwell set himself up as a publisher in Oxford, often sourcing his non-fiction reference materials from impoverished post-war Poland. Notably, he was the Labour MP for Buckingham from 1964-70. By the time he disappeared off his private yacht in 1991 (did he jump? – was he pushed?), his fully-inflated ego failing to keep his head above water, Maxwell's company had expanded to include Mirror Group Newspapers and Maxwell Communications. His frantic acquisitions during the 1970s were funded by enormous loans often based on Maxwell's exaggerated claims and force of personality.

Not only had his business concerns expanded: so had his girth. Carpenters were commissioned to build outsized lavatories for the man at his many offices. But by the late 1980s his businesses had spiralled into enormous debt. With both Maxwell and his credit rating looking decidedly unhealthy, 'Cap'n Bob' decided to raid the company's pension fund to the tune of £400 million. He went on his final swim leaving his loyal family to face the flak.

### Rich Pickings

**Thomas Coughlin** was vice-chairman of the US retail giant Wal-Mart. Over a lengthy career he amassed stock worth more than US$20 million dollars, and by the time he retired in 2005 was making over US$4 million a year in salaries and bonuses. A man with shopping in his blood, Mr. Coughlin couldn't resist topping up his nest egg with US$500,000 worth of cash, goods and company gift vouchers which he spent on himself. And that wasn't all: in a series of lawsuits brought against him by his former employers he was alleged to have falsified expense claims and filed a false tax return. Items pilfered included an all-terrain vehicle at US$10,000, a pair of handmade alligator boots at US$1,359, a US$319 fishing license, a Celine Dion CD at US$9.72 and US$3.54-worth of Polish sausage. He had joined the company in 1978 as Head of Theft Prevention.

Corporate golden boy and CEO of Tyco, multi-millionaire **Dennis Kozlowski** treated himself to the very best money could buy – except it wasn't his money, it was the company's. Most of us wouldn't know where to start looking for a US$6,000 shower curtain, a US$17,000 travelling 'toilette box' or a US$15,000 umbrella stand shaped like a poodle – and how does anyone manage to spend US$2,900 on coat hangers? In total, the son of a New Jersey police detective looted some US$135 million from the multi-national group, which he lavished on expensive properties, fine art and antiques (although in a more thoughtful moment he donated US$4 million to Cambridge University to fund a professorship in corporate governance). In 2005, however, Mr. Kozlowski found his multi-million dollar lifestyle drastically reduced when he started a new job, mopping the floors of a New York Correctional Facility for just US$1 a day. Any thoughts of early retirement were dashed in June 2009 when the Supreme Court declined to hear Mr. Kozlowski's appeal against his 8–25 year sentence for fraud.

## Black and Wife

**Conrad Black** is another self-made newpaper tycoon who won't be resuming business any time soon as he is currently a guest of the US penitentiary system. In their heyday, Baron Black of Crossharbour and his glamorous (and, it turned out, expensive) wife Barbara Amiel were the toast of society, hosting fabulous parties and splashing money about like there was no tomorrow. Black's fellow shareholders at Hollinger International began to smell a rat – the company appeared to be in trouble, so where was all that wealth coming from? A closer inspection of the accounts showed that although Hollinger was in fact making money, 95% of the entire net income was being siphoned off by a small group of senior managers, including Lord Black. When the case came before the US courts, it was revealed that he had treated his wife on expenses to US$13,935 for 'wine and champagne', and had flown her to Bora Bora on the company jet at a cost of over $565,000. These were but the tip of a very large iceberg which amounted to millions of dollars-worth of misappropriated payments, management fees and other perks, including designer handbags. Lord Black is currently in the process of preparing an appeal; in June 2009 the US Supreme Court denied him bail but have allowed him to present an appeal. Interestingly, he was also, among other things, the proprietor of the Great Expenses Scandal whistle-blower, *The Daily Telegraph*.

# J. ARTHURS

**The Cockney Rhyming Slang term refers to serial public and self-abusers. Bankers and financiers who have abused the public's trust have become two-a-penny (so to speak) in recent years.**

CHOICES ARE:

Nick Leeson

Jérôme Kerviel

Bernie Madoff

Ivan Boesky

Michael Milken

Marc Rich

Sir Fred Goodwin

Here's a list of the ones who managed to do the most damage; match their names to their deeds, and get additional points for how much money they lost, or gained:

## DAMAGE

A. Made 'insider trading' a dirty term. The line "greed is good" is attributed to him.

B. Became Chairman of NASDAQ stock exchange. Operated a Ponzi scheme described as "the biggest fraud ever committed by a single person".

C. Invented 'junk' bonds. Faced 98 counts of racketeering and securities fraud.

D. Brought about collapse of 200-year-old Barings Bank in 1995 through 'rogue trading'.

E. Destroyed Société Générale bank in 2008, through working the system of 'financial derivatives'.

F. Led rush to expand the RBS group based on financial derivatives such as sub-prime mortgage loans.

G. Invented the 'spot market' for crude oil. Indicted on tax-evasion charges, and illegal dealing with Iran during the US hostage crisis. Featured on FBI's 'Ten Most Wanted' list for several years.

**The Little Book of Big Expenses**

# GAINED

a. US$200 million and acquired "half of Beverley Hills".

b. Life of luxury in Switzerland, with US$1.5 billion to fund it. Pardon from President Clinton.

c. 150-year sentence for fraud, money laundering and perjury.

d. £700,000 per annum pension, voluntarily reduced to a mere £324,000.

e. Gaol sentence. Had film made about him. Now rehabilitated.

f. US$2.1 billion. Ranked 458th richest person in the world by Forbes magazine.

g. Still anticipates 300,000 Euro performance related bonus. Possible three-year sentence for abuse of confidence and illegal access to computers.

# Lost

i. Freedom, serving less than two years of a ten-year sentence.

ii. Freedom, serving two years of a 42-month sentence.

iii. 4.9 billion Euros.

iv. Between £16 billion and £24.9 billion.

v. An estimated US$65 billion of investor's money. Wife Ruth now ostracized — cannot have hair done or order flowers from usual suppliers.

vi. Nothing, much.

vii. Almost £1 billion.

*answers* Nick Leeson D. e. vii.; Jérôme Kerviel E. h. iii; Bernie Madoff B. c. v.; Ivan Boesky A. a. ii.; Michael Milken C.f. i.; Marc Rich G. b. vi.; Sir Fred Goodwin F. d. iv.

# BECAUSE I'M WORTH IT

**For years, one way of getting (non-taxable) extras has been widely exploited by celebrity performers, whose management will provide a list of 'contract riders' to entertainment promoters. The formula is simple: provide these extras or the star(s) will not turn up. Confronted by the inevitable, the unlucky promoter starts desperately calling up favours (usually repaid in the form of front-row tickets).**

While Australian opera singer **Dame Nellie Melba** demanded her eponymous peaches and ice cream (among other larynx lubricants) to be available on tap just off stage over a century ago, the performer who established the Gold Standard in contract riders was another 'Voice' – **Frank Sinatra**. In addition to the now bog standard 'six banqueting tables' and 'private dressing room + en suite', the crooner required a list of 'incidentals', the first page of which alone would make most people blanche (*see opposite*). The list went on for pages.

Sinatra's wasn't the only big throat that needed careful attention. Stadium opera star and famed *gourmand* **Luciano Pavarotti** required that an entire fully-stocked kitchen ("the set-up should be like at home") was made available so that he could relax while knocking up some of his favourite pasta dishes before hitting the stage (the rider adding that "there must be no distinct smells anywhere near the Artist". It also demanded a "golf cart").

Among all the tales of rock 'n' roll excess, the **Rolling Stones** probably remain the front runners, setting a template for bad-boy expense abuse on their seminal US 1969 and 1972 outings. Decades later, things ain't changed, much. Despite helpfully informing the promoters that they needn't worry: "We bring our own snooker table", the rider for a recent Stones tour insisted on specific flower arrangements involving "medium white Casablanca lilly (*sic*) and weeping eucalyptus arrangements" for Mr. Richards' and Mr.

```
Color TV (with second input for in-house video feed)
Upright piano
Private line with dedicated line, direct dial out
1 Bottle each:    Absolut or Stoli
                  Jack Daniels
                  Chivas Regal
                  Courvoisier
                  Beefeater Gin
                  White Wine – premium
                  Red Wine – premium
                  Bottled Spring Water
                  Perrier – large
Soda              Diet Coke – twenty four (24)
                  Regular Coke – twelve (12)
                  Club Soda
                  Assorted Mixers
1 Fruit Platter of sliced fresh fruit (incl. watermelon when available)
1 Cheese Tray (incl. Brie) with assorted crackers
1 Dijon Mustard
Sandwiches (Two(2)ofeach)
                  Egg Salad
                  Chicken Salad
                  Sliced Turkey
Twenty-four (24) chilled jumbo shrimp
3 cans Campbell's Chicken & Rice Soup
12 Rolls Cherry Lifesavers
12 Boxes Ludens Cough Drops – Cherry, Honey, etc.
1 Bag Miniature Tootsie Rolls
```

Wood's rooms, and constant access to satellite TV coverage of any cricket match in the world for Mr. Jagger.

But this is all far cry from the golden days when the likes of the **Grateful Dead**, **The Who** or **Led Zeppelin** were happy to settle for a few heaps of locally-scored narcotics, a busload of groupies and the opportunity to trash an hotel – all expenses paid, of course.

*"He said Mr Sinatra will be coming on just as soon as he's finished the Chivas Regal and the Nova Scotia hors d'oeuvres platter."*

## Divas

When Salome demanded John the Baptist's head on a platter she inspired a trend that is still followed by the divas of today. Egregious celebrity demands have included:

**Jennifer Lopez** Dressing room to be furnished and decked out entirely in white, and scented with expensive French candles.

**Mariah Carey** Attendant required to dispose of used chewing gum, French mineral water for bathing herself and her dog, £50,000 antique table to be flown from New York to London for autograph signing.

**Peter Gabriel** Female *masseuse* in each city of the tour to give 'a relaxing deep-muscle massage in a hippy style'. Must be able to endure 'one hour of incense-fuelled dressing room'.

The 'Artist Formerly Known As Prince' demanded that a luxury five-bedroom prefabricated house be built within the confines of the O2 Arena in London. Of course if he hadn't changed his name, he wouldn't have had to ask for this modest indulgence – they would have erected it anyway.

**Barbara Streisand** Manned metal detectors on all venue doors and rose petals in the toilet. Presumably to disguise the aroma of bullshit.

**Jim Carrey** A personal chef was required for his pet iguana during the filming of *Ace Ventura 2*. Carrey eventually agreed to split the cost of this indulgence with producers.

**Lou Reed** The noted hardened liver was concerned that 'local' organic fish, lamb, beef and chicken, manchego (or 'other sheep cheese'), calamari, and hummus and black bean dip *sans* sugar were available to him and his crew on his trans-American tour. Tough (if you're in the Midwest), but remember 'fruit must be used in small amounts and cannot be made into any kind of reduction or sauce; nothing should be fried and oil should be used sparingly'. Right, I'm waiting for the pan, Lou.

# A USER'S GUIDE TO EXPLOITING YOUR EXPENSE ACCOUNT

By now you've probably learned a fair bit from the politicians about the dark art of maximizing expenses claims. Lest we drown in self-righteousness, here are some facts and figures about the practice among humbler folk:

- Roman writing tablets discovered in 1973 near Hadrian's Wall have revealed that the practice of dipping into expenses in Britain goes back at least 2,000 years. Among the hobnails for boots and ears of grain recorded in the lists are items relating to ostentatious parties held for officers.

- In 2007, pollster YouGov conducted a survey into how many of us Brits have been tempted to embellish our expense claims. The results were eye-watering: 40% of those quizzed confessed that they would deem it acceptable to add up to 9% to the value of a claim, while a further 41% saw nothing wrong in bolstering that figure to between 10% and 25%. A select few would quite happily charge back double the full amount. Salary dissatisfaction was cited as a main cause of employees wanting to 'get back' at their bosses by bolstering their income.

- In February 2007, UK hotel chain Travelodge published details of a survey of 4,000 British workers which revealed that:

  - British workers were ripping off their employers to the tune of around a billion pounds per annum.

  - 22% admitted that they regularly fabricated their expense claims.

- The average phony claim was worth £14.60.

- Men were either a) more liable to over-claim than women, b) happier to admit to it or c) both. 27% of the males surveyed owned up, versus 18% of the fairer sex.

- 46% of British workers felt that their dodgy claims were a legitimate way of boosting their earnings.

- 59% of respondents believed that all their colleagues were 'at it'.

- Only 7% admitted to feeling guilty about inventing claims.

- 8% of businessmen confessed to claiming the cost of watching porn on hotel TV channels.

- 34% of the men had claimed for alcohol purchases.

- 42% of the women had claimed for clothing and/or accessories.

- Only 4% of respondents had been caught on the fiddle.

The top ten most popular claims were for:

> Petrol
>
> Rail tickets
>
> Food and drink
>
> Car parking
>
> Hotels
>
> Mobile phone bills
>
> Plane tickets
>
> Entertaining clients
>
> Newspapers
>
> Laundry

Some of the more egregious claims included the costs of:

Neutering a cat

Buying a hamster as a birthday present for a son

A pregnancy kit purchased after a one night stand

A masonic door knocker

Stamps for a personal collection

Dancing lessons

A family trip to Disney World

A Caribbean cruise

and…

The services of a prostitute on a business trip abroad…

When Travelodge published the results of a similar survey in April 2008, dodgy expense claims appeared to be on the increase. The average respondent was now using them to pocket an extra £17 per month, an increase of £2.40 from the 2007 figure. The items funded by the claims also seemed to have risen in outrageousness.

They included:

Plastic surgery

A diamond engagement ring

A goat (admittedly purchased for a charity)

Viagra

An office hamster called Barry

A private number plate for a BMW

The cost of a private investigator hired to find evidence to facilitate a divorce

1,000 hair extensions

The three most popular scams turned out to be:

- Asking for extra (blank) taxi receipts – most cabbies are pleased to oblige.

- Adding extra mileage when submitting claims for transport costs.

- Entertaining business clients in a cheap restaurant, then eating in an expensive one for personal pleasure and submitting the receipt from the former rather than the latter.

> * We shouldn't feel too bad though. According to a poll of 400 business travellers carried out by travel technology firm KDS in 2007, the British are a lot less liable to cheat on their expenses than some other nationalities. 21.4% of the American respondents admitted to making false claims compared with 20.6% of the French, 16.1% of the Germans and a mere 13% of the British.

### Other creative fiddles

We couldn't possibly condone any of the following. They are here for information purposes only.

- Submit receipts written in foreign alphabets. They could be for entertaining clients or they could be for a nice new handbag. Be careful not to use this technique if someone in accounts is at home in Mandarin characters or Cyrillic. It also helps if you've been abroad on business recently.

- Make up an imaginary foreign business associate to dine with (or choose an obscure one, Mr. Yamamoto, for example, was one such used by a leading London publisher) whom the accounts department are unlikely to check up on or contact for verification.

- Befriend a waiter, get him to make up an astronomical receipt and split the difference.

- Find out whether your accounts department accepts '*per diems*' (claims based on the number of days a business traveller spends away from home). US Republican Senator Sarah Palin somehow managed to wangle $16,951 worth of *per diems* from the Alaskan taxpayer for nights spent at home.

- Pick somewhere you've always wanted to go where you also happen to have a business contact. Have a five-minute meeting with them, then spend the rest of the week lying on the beach. Charge the travel expenses back to your company.

- Have lunch with a group of friends employed by various different companies. Persuade one of them to pick up the tab (and claim it on his or her expenses), then photocopy the receipt and pretend it was you. A variation is to have dinner with a group of friends. Before you order everybody makes a guess at the final bill and whoever is closest gets to take the receipt and claim it on expenses. One of the authors may conceivably have used one of these ruses in the past.

### And Finally...

Pay close attention to what the Inland Revenue has to say about tax deductible expenses, particularly if you're a company director or self-employed. The rules can get fiendishly complicated if you're a minister of religion, a fireman or similar, but in most cases the gist is as follows (taken from the HMRC website):

You can only get tax relief for allowable expenses. Expenses are allowable if they're for the cost of:

- Travelling you had to do whilst doing your job.

- Other expenses you had to pay whilst doing your job – and which related only to doing your job.

- You can't ask for tax relief if your employer has already reimbursed you for the expense and has agreed a 'dispensation' with us.

Unfortunately, 'entertaining' expenses are no longer allowable under Inland Revenue guidelines, and an extremely complex formula applies now to petrol claims, depending on the age and fuel-efficiency of your motor.

Be good and be careful.

# GLOSSARY

'For the purposes of transparency', to borrow a phrase many an MP fell back on among their desperate attempts at self-justification when the shit hit the fan, we decided to compile a list of the various terms which have now entered the English language as a result of the Great Expenses Scandal.

**ACA** – This is the now notorious **Additional Costs Allowance**, as outlined in *The Green Book*, (*see* **The Rules**) under which MPs who did not represent an inner London constituency could claim back expenses incurred 'when staying overnight away from their main UK residence... for the purpose of performing Parliamentary duties'. Under the **ACA** MPs could make claims against their second homes, including the cost of furnishings, maintenance, rent or mortgage interest and stamp duty, as well as overnight hotel accommodation. The maximum spend allowable in 2008-09 was a tax-free £24,600 per MP. Personal items, such as toiletries and clothing, were not allowed. In the 2009 edition of *The Green Book*, the **ACA** was renamed the 'Personal Additional Accommodation Expenditure', or **PAAE**.

**ACCG** – The **Additional Costs Claims Guide** was a list issued to MPs indicating what the Fees Office deemed as reasonable expenditure on certain named household items. (This became known as the 'John Lewis List'). From 2008, claiming under the **ACA** for furniture and household items was restricted before being banned altogether in May 2009.

**CGT** – **Capital Gains Tax**, payable by MPs and general public alike on any profit made from the sale of a property which was not their main home. Unless you can craftily 'flip' them.

**Dipping/double-dipping** – This generally occurred when one MP claimed against more than one property (not allowed, although a 'home office' may constitute an exception). It also cropped up in its plural form when a pair/couple of MPs individually made claims against the same property.

**Fees Office** – This body (formally the Parliamentary Fees Office) is responsible for approving (or rejecting, or at least questioning) expenses claims from MPs. The procedure evolved over the years (as did the whole allowance system), and by 2008 the amount that MPs could claim for expenses without providing receipts was slashed from £250 to just £25. In 2009, the amount of mortgage interest that MPs could reclaim was capped at £1,250 a month. From 1997, the Fees Office was run by Civil Servant Andrew Walker.

**Flipping** is when an MP changes the assignation of their 'Second Home' from one property to another, thereby enabling them to claim **ACA** for different properties. A 'Flipper' is an MP who engages in this. *The Green Book* stipulated that 'Members may only change the respective designations of main home and additional home once in any year'. In 2009, the Government announced a crackdown on the practice altogether until at least the end of 2010.

**Food Allowance** – MPs may claim up to £400 per month for food. Before April 2008 they were not required to submit receipts for this expense.

*The Green Book* – The official guide to MPs' allowances. The 2006 edition, which also included a section entitled 'Members' Salaries and Pensions', was replaced by an updated version in 2009.

**Ikea List** – In response to voters' concerns over publicized details of the **John Lewis List** in 2008, the Government placed a cap on the amount MPs could reclaim for household items, limiting it to just 10% of the total **ACA**. Dubbed the 'Ikea List', this compromise persisted until May 2009 when, after further outrage from taxpayers, MPs were prohibited from claiming at all for furniture or household goods.

**John Lewis List** – *See* **ACCG** *above*

**London Supplement** – An allowance that can be claimed by Inner London MPs instead of the **ACA**. The maximum allowed for any financial year is £22,110.

**Main Home** – Any MP whose constituency was outside Central London and who had more than one property could designate one house as their 'Main Home' and one as their 'Second Home'. The 2006 edition of *The Green Book* helpfully defined the 'Main Home' as 'the one where you spend more nights than any other'. The 2009 edition did away with the number-of-nights rule, stating simply that: 'It is for a Member to determine where his or her main home is based on his or her circumstances'.

**Office Expenses** – The costs associated with renting and maintaining a constituency office, including communications and travel, were covered by the 'Incidental Expenses Provision' of *The Green Guide*. The maximum chargeable in 2008 was £2,712.

**Second Home** – MPs were responsible for notifying the Fees Office of the location of their designated 'Second Home', as distinct from their 'Main Home', against which they could then claim expenses under the **ACA**. The 2009 edition of *The Green Book* renamed this the 'Additional Home Allowance' (AHA) and added the important stipulation that it must be in the UK. Which leads one to wonder…

**Staffing Allowance** – In 2008, a maximum of £87,276 could be reclaimed by MPs for the cost of employing office staff, whether family members or not.

**Travel Entitlements** – These were outlined in *The Green Book*. For driving costs, MPs could reclaim mileage of 40p per mile up to 10,000 miles and 25p thereafter. Even cycling MPs could claim 20p per mile. Air, rail and tube travel was also reimbursed, and MPs were able to claim the costs of up to 12 return journeys per year between their constituency and Westminster.

# INDEX

**The Little Book of Big Expenses**

ADDITIONAL ALLOWANCE BOOK PURCHASE CLAIM FORM

Title: *The Little Book of Big Expenses*

Subtitle: *How to Live the MP Lifestyle*

Authors: Unknown

Category: Reference/Humour/Business Studies/Top Shelf (*delete as required*)

ISBN: 978-1-4081-2404-8

*Purchase price:* (*please tick as appropriate*)

| | |
|---|---|
| Recommended Retail Price | ☐ |
| Amazon 'Used and New' Price | ☐ |
| High Street '3 for 2' Offer | ☐ |
| (*please indicate if it qualified as the 'free' book*) | ☐ |
| Charity Shop (specify price donated) | ☐ |
| Car Boot Sale (specify price bartered) | ☐ |

*If none of the above, please indicate which applies:*

| | |
|---|---|
| Gift | ☐ |
| Complimentary Gift from Local MP | ☐ |
| Won in Charity Auction (*name sponsor where appropriate*) | ☐ |
| Found in Street | ☐ |
| Shoplifted | ☐ |
| Complimentary Copy | ☐ |

*Reasons for Acquisition:* (*please tick as appropriate*)

| | |
|---|---|
| Business Advice | ☐ |
| Lifestyle Advice | ☐ |
| For Tax Consultant | ☐ |
| Personal Use | ☐ |

*continued overleaf*

Gift for Family Member (must be over 18) ☐

To Send to Other MP (specify party, must be over 18) ☐

Bought for 'Second Home' Bookshelf ☐

Bought for 'Main Home' Bookshelf ☐

Bought for Downstairs Loo Bookshelf ☐

Bought Because You are Named in Book ☐

Stocking Filler ☐


Total Price Paid: ☐

Purchase Tax/VAT Paid (if any): ☐


*Additional Claimable Charges*

Cost of Postage: ☐

Cost of Travel to and from Place of Purchase: ☐

Cost of Accommodation for Overnight Stay in Order to Purchase: ☐

Cost of Meals/Incidental Expenses Incurred in Purchase of this Book: ☐

Any Other Incidental Costs Associated with Purchase of this Book ☐

(Specify below in not more than 50 words)

---

Please Indicate if Receipt(s) Supplied (not essential) ☐


Claimed by (signature required) ................................................................